Make PEACE *with* MONEY

Redefine Your Relationship with Money, Master Your Personal Finances, and Discover True Wealth

LORNA MCLEOD

Make PEACE *with* MONEY: Redefine Your Relationship with Money, Master Your Personal Finances, and Discover True Wealth

Copyright © 2018 by Lorna McLeod

Publishing services provided by  **Archangel Ink**

ISBN-13: 978-1-7329062-0-4

This book is a must read for anyone who wants a more powerful, purposeful relationship with money. Being clear, positive, and at peace with finances is especially valuable for people in sales. Those who have learned to identify and shift limiting beliefs and to construct a meaningful vision are happier and more effective sellers. This very readable book, based on the author's extensive coaching experience and her own story, offers specific guidance both for internal work and for the practical nuts and bolts of money.

It will get you where you want to go.

—Carol Costello, author of The Soul of Selling
www.soulofselling.com

Your Free Resource

Before you begin reading this book, I have a free bonus for you.

In addition to the information provided in this book, I have created a *Make Peace with Money Workbook*. It is intended to help you make step-by-step changes in your thoughts, beliefs and actions that can bring genuine peace about money.

To receive your free workbook, sign up here:
www.makepeacewithmoney.com

As the *Peace with Money* community grows, I'll continue to share blog posts with additional strategies on this topic, pending programs and services, and alert you when content is updated. By subscribing you will be first in line for future giveaways and exclusive deals. I promise not to inundate you with emails, I will never share your contact information with others, and you can unsubscribe at any time.

Immediately after you sign up you'll be sent an email with access to the bonus material.

—Lorna McLeod

Dedication

To my mother, Lois Mary Starr McLeod, poet, writer, and artist, who taught me to trust myself and others.

To my beloved husband, Daniel, who has been willing to hold the energy of peace for me when I have struggled.

I am so wealthy in their love.

Disclaimer

Many of the stories in this book are about real client situations, and though the names, places, and identifying characteristics have been changed to protect client confidentiality, the situations and how they were resolved are true to each experience.

Foreword

Most people have sought for years to live a peaceful life and bring more harmony to those around them. Yet I've observed that peace with money is often a sticking point to attaining a completely balanced life.

The book you hold was written by someone who has sought, and finally found, deep peace in her own life with regards to her money, personal relationships, physical health and mental vitality. She has coupled her personal experiences with her ability as a masterful coach to offer *Make Peace with Money*. Read it and you will discover how to transform your own relationship with money into one filled with a joyous recognition of promise and possibility.

Lorna McLeod is a compassionate and exceptional guide, coach and mentor, whom I've known for nearly 30 years. She has woven together a unique blend of practical steps to change painful thoughts into positive ones, as well as hands-on exercises to address the kinds of money challenges we all face. She understands the spiritual principles that are the foundation of gaining harmony and peace in your life.

Many people think of money as a necessary evil or as that which holds them back from achieving their aims. Growing up, many, if not all of us, learned beliefs or patterns of thinking that get in the way of having a happy, harmonious life, especially with money. Here are some examples. "I'm bad with money." "Money is bad (or evil, or the root of all evil)." "There's never enough money and there will never be enough money." Few of us have ever learned how to change our thinking to escape these patterns.

Lorna gives you stories about situations that she, her clients and her acquaintances have experienced. As she does this, you'll see how to open new lines of thought about your own finances.

What do you want to do with your money? How much of it would you like to have? First, you'll see how to do well with the money you have, and then how to define what you truly want to accomplish with your money. It is through clarity about who you are and what you want in life that you can design the role of money in that vision. And if you find you do want more, you'll have a clearer idea of how much you require and how to create ways to attain it. Then you will have genuine satisfaction and reward from getting it.

Something interesting occurs when you get completely clear about your financial objectives and begin to live by that clarity. You will likely become much happier about your relationship with money, and you'll begin to see ways you can earn or bring in more financial good into your life.

Many people are waking up to the fact that everything they need to be successful is already inside of themselves, just waiting to be unleashed. Sometimes, though, all that is needed is a guide to remind us of that fact, and to help us clear a path to get there. This is where the support of a book like *Make Peace with Money* comes in.

In the last analysis, if your desire is for more peace in the world, then this step toward peace in your own life, with money, may be the most powerful one you can make.

Maria Nemeth, Ph.D. MCC
Author of *Mastering Life's Energies*
Founder, Academy for Coaching Excellence

Acknowledgements

I am deeply grateful to all of my family members, friends, teachers, mentors, and spiritual guides who have demonstrated peaceful living in their own lives and encouraged me to seek peace in mine.

Of particular note is Coach Maria Nemeth, Ph.D., founder of the Academy for Coaching Excellence, for her unyielding knowing that seeking to have a healthy relationship with money can be a powerful pathway for healing and well-being every aspect of ourselves. Her books, *The Energy of Money and Mastering Life's Energies*, sit by my desk for easy reference and are recommended reading for all my clients.

Evonne Ryan, financial coach and mentor, introduced me to financial coaching for my own benefit and showed me the sheer joy of supporting others to have breakthroughs with money. Her coaching brought me my own first experience of true peace with money. Evonne introduced me to master coach Joan King, now deceased, whose clarity of thought about coaching improved my skills immensely. Also to Nancy Smyth of the Arbinger Institute, which published the landmark book, *The Anatomy of Peace*, a powerful guide to creating peace in relationships with others.

A special note of gratitude goes to Julia Petrisor, outstanding author and editor, whose contribution to this book was of enormous support through a period when I needed it most. It is a significantly better book because I was willing to engage with her assistance. And to fellow coach, Shelley Hannah, whose nearly daily coach buddy sessions kept me focused and on track with this project.

Thanks go to all of the coaches from the Licensed Trainers group of the Academy for Coaching Excellence, who variably held my feet to the fire when I was lagging on this *Peace with Money* project and who figuratively held my hand when I was feeling uncertain. I especially want to thank LAT coach/trainers Carolyn Rose Hart, Jeremy Blanchard, Kris Thaller, Lori Gorrell, Zo Tobi, Wayne Manning and Beth Ann Suggs.

I've been graced to have a group of women friends, the Wilderness Women, about twenty of us, who have been backpacking, pot-lucking, celebrating, and mourning together since the late 1970s. We've all benefited so much through the nurturing of this collective relationship. Though scattered across several states, we harmonize well not only when singing together, but also in our lives as a whole. I reside in peace from your friendship, my dear friends, you know who you are. Thank you so very much!

Peace doesn't occur in a vacuum. Certainly peace with money takes communication, cooperation, and a real desire to achieve it. There are so many others who have contributed to my peace with money and to the contents of this book, from my bankers, to my spouse, to my friends, that it would be impossible to name you all.

My web designer, Zachary Stark Macmillan, has been with me from the start of this project and contributed immensely to the clarity of my web site. And he's a joy to work with as well.

It is with heartfelt delight I give credit to my team at Archangel Ink, including project manager Kristie Lynn, marketing and launch guru Jordan Ring, editor extraordinaire Nichole Kraft, and the rest of the team that made the production of this book move along so smoothly. It would have been so much more difficult without your expertise.

Last yet certainly not least, I acknowledge the many hundreds of clients I've coached since 1990. You have been so willing to generously share your challenges and your celebrations. You've clarified the life you desire and have sought out and addressed the debris that got in the way of achieving your dreams. And you've let me walk this path toward peace with you. I've learned so much from and with you. I am grateful.

Namaste.

—Lorna

CONTENTS

As You Begin...1

Chapter 1: Peace with Money...9

Chapter 2: Are You at War with Money?..23

Chapter 3: Disarming the War with Money....................................35

Chapter 4: Becoming Conscious about Your Money......................47

Chapter 5: Building a Positive Relationship with Money...............61

Chapter 6: Moving from Insufficiency to Sufficiency....................77

Chapter 7: A Positive Relationship with Money............................89

Chapter 8: Discovering the Purpose You Want Your Money to Serve....105

Chapter 9: Bringing Your Vision for Your Money Alive.................119

Chapter 10: Choosing Ease over Struggle with Money................131

Chapter 11: Peace Increases with Certainty................................151

Chapter 12: Who Is Your Team? 163

Chapter 13: Celebrate!...173

Chapter 14: Upping the Ante: Making Peace in the World...........181

Thank You..189

A Quick Favor Please?...191

About the Author...193

AS YOU BEGIN . . .

Do you want to be more effective and happier with your money? Would you prefer to spend more of your precious time and energy fulfilling your dreams and less of it worrying about money issues? In effect, would you like to have a more harmonious relationship with money?

This is my dream for you, a desire that grew out of my own life experience.

Throughout my childhood and middle teenage years, I was quite good with money. I knew to the penny how much I had in my piggy bank because I counted it every week. I also knew exactly how much I had in my pocket and in my savings account.

I knew how much money I earned for each chore and which additional tasks around the farm I could do to earn extra income when I wanted it. Whenever I desired something, I found out what it would cost, saved for it, and bought it with cash. I was also able to do fairly complex math problems in my head, so I certainly was not afraid of numbers. The only time I recall being stressed about money was when I was about five years old. I stole a tiny toy piggy from the five-and-dime store. My mom found it and took me back to the store to return it and apologize. Oh, how hard it was to open my mouth and make amends for what I'd done.

At the age of thirteen, I started milking cows for my dad and, within a couple of years, for other local dairy farmers. By the time

I was seventeen, my work had earned enough money to buy and breed a small herd of dairy cattle that became my main financial support for college.

At seventeen I married a man who had very little confidence in himself; it was almost as if he made it a mission to undermine my self-confidence as well. During the four years of that marriage, I became deeply unsure about many aspects of myself, including my ability to handle money. I don't really blame him. I was the one who let it happen. Nonetheless, I suddenly wasn't so sure how to earn money, how to spend it, or how to save it. I began telling myself that I was bad with money and, consequently, that I was bad with numbers.

I continued telling this story to myself for most of my younger adult years, long after that relationship ended. Throughout those years, even while I was growing in understanding of how to have a harmonious and peace-filled life, as well as becoming an advocate of peace for others, money was the one area where I consistently struggled.

As you may surmise, something similar happens to a lot of people. They have never learned how to handle money effectively or something happens that shakes their confidence and they get off track. They tell themselves a story that simply isn't true, yet they believe it anyway.

They might tell a story that they are entitled to have whatever they want, whenever they want it. So they buy on credit and go deeply into debt. Or they think they don't have enough—and will never have enough—so why bother keeping track? They may be so unsure about how to handle money that whenever they think about it, they experience dread or terror at the thought. Or they may think that money isn't virtuous, so a person should not have

2

a lot of it. Or they could be wrestling with something else that gets in the way of a healthy relationship with money.

In my case, I simply started telling myself I was bad with money. Then I gathered evidence that what I was telling myself was true. You can imagine how adversely this story affected my monetary decisions.

After a number of years of being ill at ease to the point of dread with money, I experienced a financial crisis. I was downsized out of my job and found myself unemployed. At the same time, my husband was experiencing stress-related health issues that turned out to be multiple sclerosis. He needed to find a less demanding job. Whereas before we were making a very comfortable living between the two of us, we now found we had lost about 65 percent of our income. We were nearly impoverished.

Prior to these events, we had made a number of high-risk investments in the interest of building our retirement savings quickly. Shortly after I became unemployed, we were caught in the storm as the dot-com bubble burst. We lost about 85 percent of our savings. Although we worked hard to avoid it, within a couple of years we had to declare bankruptcy.

I swore to myself, "Never again. I'm never again going to be in this place and in this relationship with money."

Though I could hardly afford it, I hired a financial coach. She supported me to become completely clear about my financial situation as it stood right then. She guided me to articulate a new vision for my life and money so I could move past the pain and conflict I'd been experiencing. She helped me determine my life priorities. I created some achievable goals and a series of small-step actions to help change our circumstances.

The most important aspect is that I engaged my husband in helping bring about these changes. While he wasn't a devotee of coaching, he'd seen me get good results in other areas of my life, including our relationship. Rather reluctantly, he said he was willing to participate because he, too, wanted an end to the financial struggles. We had some real challenges as we looked at our quite different aims for our careers. He needed less stressful work and fewer hours, while I was fully engaged in my coaching career. Because we've always put harmony in our relationship first, however, we agreed that I would take the lead and he would engage with me to gain harmony with money too.

In an early conversation, I told my coach I was apprehensive about whether my husband and I could change our situation. I told her I was bad with money and bad with numbers. She gave me a worksheet so I could compile the facts of my current financial condition.

It was empowering to become absolutely clear about where my husband and I were with money right at that moment. I stated exactly how much we owed, got a realistic value of what we owned, determined what was in the bank, and gathered other facts about our money.

When we met for my next coaching session, my coach reviewed my finances. Then she uttered some of the most empowering words I've ever heard: "Lorna, looking at these records, and recalling what you've told me, I see that you aren't actually bad with money or numbers. There are simply some things about money you don't know yet."

"Wow!" I said to myself. "Simply some things I don't know yet..."

One thing I do know about myself is that I love to learn. "So," I thought, "if I don't know those things yet, I can certainly learn them."

My coach asked me, "Lorna, would you be willing, just for this week, to stop saying that you're bad with money and numbers?"

Although I wasn't sure whether I could do it, I agreed to try. I stopped telling myself that story—just for those few days. And an odd thing happened: it felt so good not telling myself that old story that I just kept going.

Even now, occasionally, the timeworn thought comes up, "Oh, I can't do that because I'm bad with money." But I never let it stick. I simply say to myself, "Okay. I'm pretty good with money and I love to learn, so what is it I don't know yet? And where can I learn about it?"

The day my coach told me there were simply some things I didn't know about money is also the day I decided to become a financial coach. I thought, "If I could help others have the peace of mind my coach just gave me, now *that* would be joyous work."

I think of this shift in my self-talk as a crucial step toward learning to make peace with money. My own money story has been interwoven with my interest in learning to have a peaceful life overall. This couples well with my desire to support efforts for peace in the world. This book is the synthesis of these interests, melding financial coaching with my life passion to be a harbinger of peace. When we have peace with money, it extends outward into our lives and contributes to greater peace on the planet.

This book is meant to be enjoyed by reading it in its entirety; however, you can also pick it up, skim it, and reference it time and again for actions that can help your situation in the present moment. The exercises for each chapter build on the previous chapter if you approach the work systematically, yet they can also be worked effectively as individual exercises.

The book's framework rests on the concept that when we want change, we must discover what we desire to create, secure a way of being and thinking that supports the change we want, and take action to follow through. Thus, the book walks you through creating your vision for monetary peace, examines how warring with money shows up in our lives, and offers choices you can make and actions you can take to achieve peace with money.

The first three steps begin with building a conscious frame of mind toward money, one that is positive and affirming, full of encouraging thoughts and gratitude. You will use the foundation of this reframed mind-set to create a purposeful vision.

The final three steps take you deeper into action backed by purpose, with practical exercises to implement your vision. You'll learn to recognize and embrace the value of engaging support from others while you do this work.

The final two chapters invite you to celebrate the work you have done and the progress you've made and, indeed, to integrate a spirit of gratitude and celebration into your life.

You are also invited to up the ante and allow your newfound peace with money to expand across all aspects of your life, paving the way for you to truly become a beacon of peace. For some, this will mean becoming an activist or advocate for justice, freedom, or some other worthy cause. For others, it will be simply to be that beacon of peace for those closest to us. Our world needs both.

Finding peace with money is a gift you can give yourself. In view of the struggles we encounter in our lives as human beings, it is essential that we find and create as much mental and emotional ease for ourselves and others as we can. It is my sincere hope that by actively using this book, you will change your troubled relationship with money to one that brings peace and ease, allowing you to truly savor life in all its joy and richness.

Chapter 1
PEACE WITH MONEY

Possession of material riches without inner peace is like dying of thirst while bathing in a lake.

—Paramahansa Yogananda

If we truly want to change this tumultuous world into a more peaceful one, we must initially make the change within ourselves. If we truly want to renegotiate our troubled relationship with money to one that is peaceful, we must cultivate peace within ourselves in a strategic way. Whether you are just beginning to walk a path toward peace or have embraced peace for years and yet are not at peace with money, the first step toward peace with money is to decide that you want it.

Money has evolved over time to become the most significant and commonly used means of energetic exchange across the planet. Yet, for all its seeming importance and power, few of us feel at ease with either the topic or money itself—nor do we feel at peace when considering money in relation to ourselves.

It's a sobering truth that many people who feel a lack of peace with money actually have enough of it to meet all their basic financial needs. Where many go awry is the material culture we live in. We take on a belief that we want more, and then still more, without regard to the impact those acquisitions have on our peace of mind. We believe more belongings and more money equals more happiness, yet studies measuring happiness show this isn't true.[1] Many who are ill at ease about money simply have not learned how to live well and happily with it. While there is nothing intrinsically wrong with having belongings, it's the cost they can bring to our peace of mind that we seek to address.

Through coaching with clients both in the United States and internationally, I've found that many in the world feel a strong degree of discomfort with money. Throughout my explorations, I've found it matters less how *much* money you have than it does how you think about it, how you feel about it, and what you do with it. I have been intrigued to discover that many people who live on extremely small amounts of money have less stress about the lack of it than do those who have a lot. These people have learned how to live well with little.

Monetary comfort (or discomfort) comes down to how a person manages their beliefs and internal chatter, how clear their vision is for their lives, and how they actually handle their money. Rich or poor, far too many people needlessly feel ill at ease with money.

As a financial coach and lover of peace, I have come to see that the most fundamental shift people can make to change their relationship with money is to *learn* to be at peace with it.

You may say, "But Lorna, I don't want some warm and fuzzy feeling. I want money in the bank!" I assure you that once peace is present, you'll almost certainly experience greater ease with money in several ways. You'll know clearly where you stand with money so you can make more effective decisions about it. Better decisions usually mean the money begins to flow more readily.

---

1   Carolyn Gregoire, "The Psychology of Materialism, and Why It's Making You Unhappy," *HuffPost*, December 15, 2013, https://www.huffingtonpost.com/2013/12/15/psychology-materialism_n_4425982.html.

Don't get me wrong—this is not a get-rich-quick book. Other resources can lead you in that direction if that is what you prefer. Should you wish to go that direction, however, I urge you to realize that get-rich-quick approaches usually involve a good deal of risk, often along with very long hours at work. Instead, this book is about creating a strong, sustainable relationship with money in which you can also experience ease and harmony.

If you choose to take an honest assessment of your life and your relationship to money, consider this: What is it you really want?

You may say, "That's easy. I want to be a millionaire." Yet I know a number of multimillionaires who don't feel at all secure about their wealth, who are driven to earn more and more. They are terrified of losing what they have and therefore fail to enjoy their money or their lives. If I were to press you, we just might find that what you truly want is to simply feel a sense of plenty, ease, and harmony about your financial situation—to have the sense that you have enough. You may find that in order to experience a sense of ease and harmony, you'll need to bring in more, spend less, or spend in different ways. Or perhaps all of these.

You'll find that money itself is rarely, if ever, the only or final solution to a problem. By making the effort to examine and then work with your opinions, conclusions, feelings, and actions toward money, you can change your life in profound ways.

This is the journey of discovery we'll take together if you are willing, the journey of learning to feel at peace with the money you already have and the dollars you'll continue to earn and spend. You'll also lay the groundwork for more effective decision making for yourself and greater harmony in your monetary relationships with others.

Before we dive into this transformative discussion, it is crucial we reveal what peace is and how we refer to it throughout the book.

Over the years, I've studied in person with a number of thought leaders. These include Nancy Smyth of the Arbinger Institute; Maria Nemeth;[2] Mary Mackenzie of Peace Workshop International; and Evonne Ryan.[3] I've also studied the teachings of Pema Chödrön;[4] Marshall Rosenberg;[5] Eckhart Tolle;[6] and numerous others through coursework and webinars.

Each of the preceding people has stated that it is unrealistic to think we can be in a peaceful state of mind 100 percent of the time. We are, after all, human beings. The aim is not to avoid conflict at all costs but to come to a place where we quickly recognize when we are struggling and then take remedial action immediately to bring us back (or forward) into a state of harmony.

When I'm coaching people to address their financial situation and be happier and more effective with money, they rarely, if ever, initially speak about what they want in terms of peace. They know they are conflicted. They want respite from that struggle. Yet, often, when I speak about the possibility that they could go

---

2   I highly recommend Maria Nemeth's wonderful book *Mastering Life's Energies: Simple Steps to a Luminous Life at Work and Play* (Novato, CA: New World Library, 2007).

3   I studied under financial coach Evonne Ryan at her College for Financial Coaching in Littleton, Colorado from 2005–2008.

4   Pema Chödrön, *Getting Unstuck: Breaking Your Habitual Patterns and Encountering Naked Reality*, read by the author (Louisville, CO: Sounds True, 2005).

5   Marshall B. Rosenberg, *Nonviolent Communication: A Language of Life* (Encinitas, CA: PuddleDancer Press, 2003).

6   Eckhart Tolle, *The Power of Now: A Guide to Spiritual Enlightenment* (Novato, CA: New World Library, 1999). More information about Tolle and his teachings can be found at www.eckharttolle.com.

beyond merely a sense of relief to experience actual peace, they light up. The liberation they feel, even at the mere idea of peace with money, is palpable. As one client said, "If I've never thought about a harmonious relationship with money before, how can I ever hope to stop struggling? It's such a habit, fighting with myself and others about money. Half the time I don't even know I'm doing it."

As you progress through the book, you will be invited to see clearly where you struggle with money and also notice where you experience peace with it, even if only for a moment. I'll offer methods to help you identify your challenges and ways to bring yourself into harmony. But first, so you have a benchmark, let's explore how peace with money might look.

Peace is most often defined as the absence of war or conflict.

While there are other definitions related to societies or nations as a whole, including "freedom from civil clamor and confusion," and "a pact or agreement to end hostilities," the definitions most pertinent to the effort of gaining peace with money according to the *Merriam-Webster Unabridged Dictionary* are: (1) "a mental or spiritual condition marked by freedom from disquieting or oppressive thoughts or emotions"; (2) "harmony in human or personal relations"; and (3) a state "that makes, gives, or maintains tranquility."[7]

Defining Peace Relative to Money

Peace with money is the overall ability to be relaxed, to have a sense of tranquility when thinking about, communicating about, or taking actions in regard to money. My purpose here is

---

7   *Merriam-Webster Unabridged Dictionary*, s.v. "peace (*n.*)," accessed August 27, 2018, http://unabridged.merriam-webster.com/unabridged/peace.

to help you learn concrete, practical tools for living peacefully with money day-to-day. A good place to begin is by exploring the degree of peace you are experiencing with yourself right now.

Peace with Self

How you experience peace currently, with yourself and in your relationships, will set the tone for how you experience peace with money. However, the converse is also true. As you establish a peace-filled relationship with money, you will likely find yourself experiencing greater harmony overall with yourself and others.

It is unrealistic to expect that you will feel peaceful all of the time, especially if this work is new to you. However, much like any practice, peace is a state of mind you can develop. You'll move beyond just noticing the moments when you feel peaceful to a place where you'll actively choose to feel peace.

The difference between a thought that just comes up and actively choosing a thought is significant, and the practice is surprisingly simple. As simple, in fact, as choosing which thought brings you more peace. Which thought is more peaceful: "I'm afraid that bill will get there too late so I have to call the payment in now," or "Since this bill is due next week, I'll pay it right now so that it's taken care of."

Josh noticed that when he thought about putting off paying his bills until just before they were due, he felt anxious that he could miss the due date and have to pay a late penalty. When he thought to pay his bills in advance of the due date, he felt a strong degree of certainty about his actions and the anxious feeling went away. Josh saw that thinking and acting promptly brought him greater peace.

When Marilyn decided to help her daughter furnish her college dorm room, she felt good about supporting her daughter but conflicted because if she spent as much as she intended to, it would leave her short for her house payment that month. And while she didn't want to add more to her already-quite-full credit card, she also didn't want to disappoint her daughter. When she confessed her mixed feelings, her daughter said, "Mom, I've been saving and I can put in more than $400." Marilyn felt greater monetary ease and at the same time built clarity and reasonable expectations with her daughter.

What action in this moment will bring more peace to you and others involved? The foundation for finding peace with money comes from finding peace with yourself—peace with how you are in the world, peace with the decisions you make, peace with how you engage in relationships and show up for others.

If all this feels new and as though it could be a lot of work, I assure you it does not have to be. The two—peace with your thoughts and peace with money—go hand in hand. The more you choose peace within yourself, the easier it becomes to choose peace with your money. And the more you choose peace when thinking about and managing your money, the more peace you'll have within yourself.

Think of a time when you felt wholly at peace, even if it was only for a moment or two. Perhaps you were gazing at a lovely sunset. Or maybe you were listening to a trickling brook or smelling a lily or freshly baked bread. Or maybe you were hearing a loved one laugh or receiving a hug from a friend.

What do you notice as you think about peace now? Do you feel calmer? More at ease? Or does the mere word "peace" contrast with your life so much so that you feel a sense of unrest? To come to a place of peace with money, it's vital that you allow yourself to be authentic (perhaps even vulnerable) about how you feel and what you see about yourself and money.

It is through observing what isn't working for us, along with what is going well, that we discern the choices we want to make. Observing what we are thinking and how we are behaving allows us to gain greater clarity about ourselves. We can see what we want and also what we don't want. By turning toward what we do want, we can shift into more effectiveness, more peace, more of what we want. This observation also encourages us to move away from thoughts and actions that produce anxiety, worry, or stress.

Peace with Self around Money

While I encourage you to be rigorous in exploring this topic of peace with money, I also urge you to be compassionate toward yourself. More than likely, you've made mistakes with money. Maybe even some really big ones. Here's the good news: you are in excellent company. I've made mistakes with money, some that have cost me tens of thousands of dollars. And, after working with hundreds of people, I've come to realize that pretty much everyone else has too. Yet, more than likely, you've also made some excellent choices with money. You'll get to see and celebrate those, too, as you begin to shift your relationship with money from one of struggle to one of ease.

The difference between those who continue to struggle with money and those who don't is that those who don't have chosen to focus on how they desire their lives to be. They take time to become clear about what works and what doesn't. Then they make the effort to change attitudes, habits, and ways of talking about money. Notably, they have changed their actions and behaviors with money.

The more aware you become of the peaceful moments in your life as a whole, the more likely you will be to seek them out. Growing your peaceful self has many benefits, among them less stress, better health, an improved sense of well-being, and greater harmony in relationships with others.

Connecting Peace with Self to Peace with Money

Growing peace with money, likewise, has numerous benefits.

For many years, when I sat down with my spouse or a business partner to work on finances, I'd be so nervous that I'd pick a fight, or I'd be so reticent about discussing what I'd spent and what I'd earned that my partner would become frustrated or angry. In either situation, there was clearly no harmony or accord in the room.

For a person who prided herself on being a good wife and an excellent business partner, this was a glaring gap. Sadly, I simply did not see that I was responsible for at least half of the situation. More than half, really, because usually I had bought something I hadn't told my husband about or was secretive about something I was afraid he would not approve of. I thought battling about money was the only way to handle it. I'd seen similar battles between my mom and dad, who had otherwise been happily married. I thought the arguments were inevitable.

Among my women friends, I heard similar stories about their money dealings with their partners. It was my financial coach who brought to my attention that there are many couples who have genuine harmony in their financial relationships. She spoke of clients who had worked through problems with monetary communications and who had extraordinary harmony between them regarding their finances.

I became immensely curious about how this could possibly be. It seemed so foreign to me. My coach helped me see that any effort to heal my relationship with others about money would, of necessity, begin with me. I must come to a place of greater peace within myself before seeking to change the situation with others.

She encouraged me to notice when I tensed up while dealing with money. I saw that the worst times were when I thought about paying bills with my husband (even more so than when we were actually paying them). With my coach's encouragement, I began to think about how I would like to feel instead. Did I want to feel calm? Focused? At ease? I learned to take a few minutes to think about the feelings I desired to experience before I met with my husband.

Instead of waiting to pay bills until the last minute, we began to schedule time to plan our finances and pay bills twice each month. How I dreaded those bimonthly meetings at first. Yet I was determined to change my attitudes about money in order to gain greater ease. At first, I couldn't even think about peace with money. It was enough to simply take myself by the hand and not antagonize my partner. This was the "absence of conflict" definition of peace.

After several months, I began noticing that I was feeling quite calm all the way through our money meetings. While I had not yet achieved real tranquility or peace, I was rarely struggling. As our communication became less strife-ridden, I noticed my husband was calmer during our meetings as well. We began to make better decisions about money, ones that supported a simpler yet significantly happier lifestyle overall.

The practice of choosing ahead of time how I wanted to feel while engaged with money tasks, both with myself alone and with my partner, eventually led to the tranquility I'd been seeking. I have to admit, it took a good while of practice to come from all-out conflict to the harmony I experience most of the time now. Perhaps I'm a slow learner; however, I can unequivocally say that it is worth every bit of the time and practice I put into it.

Peace with money is clearly something you are interested in or you would not be reading this book. The chapters that follow will help expand your view of what peace with money might be like for you. Exercises, tools, and coaching questions at the end of each section— and in the companion workbook—aim to support your adventure and shift to a more peaceful relationship with money. I wish you well on your journey.

Peace with Money Activities

- Begin keeping a "peace with money" notebook or journal. This can be as simple as jotting down a few words when you think about what you want with money, peace, or both. It can be a place where you answer questions and do the exercises from each chapter. Create one location, online or in a notebook, where you keep record of the work you do to reduce stress and anxiety about money.

- Think about money for a few moments. What are you experiencing? Notice if there is a place in your body you feel something. What is happening? Consciously make an effort to relax that part of your body. Breathe in gently and deeply. Let your breath out slowly. Breathing gently is one action you can take when you start to tense up or feel anxious about money.

- Is there another practice that helps you relax? For some, it's a brisk walk outside. For others, it may be a sip of water or a good body stretch. What is your preferred way to shift to a sense of greater well-being? Practice it whenever you notice you are feeling uneasy about money.

- Think about your choices with money. You can likely point out some mistakes you've made. Write down one or two. You may begin to feel tense when you do this, so do your relaxation practice while you are writing.

- Now look to see where you have made one or more first-rate choices about money, choices you know were good ones. Write those down. And right now, take your hand, reach over your shoulder, and pat yourself on the back for the quality of your choice. Then decide how you will acknowledge that success.

- Each time you have a success, acknowledge yourself for it. From time to time, actively celebrate. This can be as simple as taking an extra few minutes on your drive home from work to look at a lovely garden or strolling through the local park that you rarely take time to enjoy. It doesn't need to cost money, although it could. One of my favorites is a cup of Mexican cocoa from my local barista. I save it, though, for celebrations so it remains special rather than becoming mundane.

Additional Resources

- Refer to the free *Make Peace with Money Workbook* at www.makepeacewithmoney.com, Lesson 1. Log in with the username *makepeacewithmoney* and the password *peace42*.

- *The Anatomy of Peace: Resolving the Heart of Conflict* by the Arbinger Institute (2nd ed.).

Chapter 2

ARE YOU AT WAR WITH MONEY?

The most fundamental aggression to ourselves, the most fundamental harm we can do to ourselves, is to remain ignorant by not having the courage and the respect to look at ourselves honestly and gently.

—Pema Chödrön

To come to a place of peace with money, we must make a conscious choice to systematically examine our beliefs, thoughts, and conclusions about it. We must recognize the thoughts and actions that keep us at war with money. In other words, where does the discord show up for us as individuals? It is only through this self-reflection that we can choose to behave differently with money.

Maria Nemeth, author of *Mastering Life's Energies*, says, "Financial success is doing what you said you would do with money, consistently, with clarity, focus, ease, and grace."[8] This definition is a good prescription for discovering peace with money, as well. Yet I wonder: How many of us have actually declared clearly and confidently what we intend to do with our money? How explicit are you about your intentions? In other words, have you become crystal clear about what you want with money? Have you determined what success with money would actually look like for you? Asking these questions of yourself leads to clarity, a

---

8   Maria Nemeth, *Mastering Life's Energies: Simple Steps to a Luminous Life at Work and Play* (Novato, CA: New World Library, 2007), 14.

principle we'll be talking about throughout this book. By *clarity*, I mean that your intent can be easily understood—without obscurity or ambiguity.

Look and see: How do you keep yourself in conflict with money? In what ways do you let your relationship with money drain your mental, emotional, and physical resources? In fact, how do you persist in being at war with money?

If you're not clear about what you want, it is unlikely you will experience the ease and grace Nemeth speaks about. Once you have clarity, it becomes much easier to stay focused on what you want and then take action accordingly. Actions derived from a clear view of what you want have a certain coherence that contributes to peace of mind. When you take actions with little intentional thought or focus, the result usually brings you into a state of chaos and war with yourself—and potentially, with others closest to you.

Take a look: When you make spur-of-the-moment financial decisions or spend on something because your peers are and you don't want to be left out, do these actions bring you peace?

When you let money control you (rather than the other way around), you are more apt to feel like you are being driven rather than being the driver. You'll feel powerless. Further, the incoherence between these driven actions and a well-thought-out plan for your money leads to anxiety. It's difficult for the seeds of financial peace to be planted.

You may ask, "How can I get to that state of peace or ease with money when I'm struggling so much right now?" Although this chapter details the effects of being at war with money, the rest of this book lays out a path to come to peace with it. As one of my students recently said upon finishing the Make Peace with Money course, "There were times I wanted to drop out. Looking at my current status was awful! Yet I'm so glad I stayed with it. I'm gaining greater peace about money than I ever thought possible. I'm looking forward to even greater peace."

Few things in life are as exhausting as being in conflict with ourselves. The Arbinger Institute, in its book *The Anatomy of Peace*, says that when we are in conflict with ourselves "our hearts are at war."[9] Fighting with ourselves drains energy, clouds our thinking, and tends to make us feel angry or depressed. Under the effects of these emotions, we cannot be at our best with ourselves, much less with those around us. We are unlikely to make clear, sensible decisions about money, and are even less likely to take sound action with it.

When we are not happy with the decisions we make or the actions we take, we tend to feel animosity toward ourselves. When this internal strife revolves around money, we often bleed that stress outward into our relationships. Not satisfied to be at war alone, we take hostages with us.

Most of us believe money in and of itself has some sort of meaning. We may think of it as bad or good, evil or magical, wonderful or awful. How we think about its meaning differs from situation to situation, based on the specific purpose money has for us at the moment.

When we contribute to a cause or purpose we deeply believe in—for example, a charitable organization—our use of money takes on an aura of goodness.

---

9   The Arbinger Institute, *The Anatomy of Peace: Resolving the Heart of Conflict*, 2nd ed. (Oakland: Berrett-Koehler, 2015), 31.

When we have to "pay the bills" or own up to a poor financial decision we've made, we feel burdened or frustrated and the meaning of money shifts with those feelings. This is especially true if we don't have enough to pay our bills in full, plus pay for groceries, shelter, utilities, clothing, and the "goodies" we want.

The High Cost of Being at War with Money

The minimum cost of being at war with money is a lack of well-being within and toward oneself. Beyond that, there are other costs. Underlying uncertainty brings a feeling of insecurity. You may believe you can't trust yourself or others. You may not feel supported by others in regard to your financial decisions, or you may question your ability to support yourself, or lack faith that you have enough. You feel powerless, a slave to money or victim to some mysterious money machinations you don't understand.

A feeling of conflict, a sense that money is the enemy, presides over your financial interactions. Alternatively, you may feel a sense of entitlement, as if some person, group of people, or the world owes you a living.

A high cost of being at war with money is that such struggles draw in innocent bystanders. These could be your parents, spouse or life partner, friends, or other relatives. Too often, it's young children who don't know how to deflect hostility, so they assume your behavior is just a way of being with money. This teaches a whole new generation to be at war with money.

Many a marriage or life partnership has foundered on the shoals of money disagreements. A January 2017 survey from the credit bureau Experian "shows that nearly 60 percent of divorcees admit that money played some role in their breakup," according to an article by Dori Zinn. "In relationships where finances played a major role, most blame their spouse's spending and debt. Rod Griffin, director of public education for Experian, says it's those couples that didn't even talk about money to begin with," Zinn writes.[10]

In relationships such as these, one or both parties may have had little experience with creating and living within a budget. Or they may have had debt from before the relationship that they did not adequately resolve before partnering up. Sadly, one partner may blame the other because, usually, we don't want to own up to our part in the situation. Not knowing how, we are often reluctant to take the initiative to change.

Many a parent has disowned a child, or children have estranged themselves from parents, through wars with money. The warring parties don't know how to stop the fight and learn to agree. A sense of shame about not knowing what to do about or with money gets in the way of seeking help to resolve monetary issues.

As nations have known for eons, coming to peace from a state of war takes effort—usually a lot of effort. It begins with a conscious decision by the warring parties to seek accord. The effort toward peace almost always comes from the decision of one party that they've had enough fighting. They decide to engage with the other party, who realizes they also have had enough and are ready for a change. Let's look at the components of peace with money. One or more of these components may spark ideas about where you can begin your path to peace.

---

10   Dori Zinn, "Couples Aren't Talking About Money in Marriage," Debt.com, March 16, 2017, https://www.debt.com/2017/couples-arent-talking-money-marriage.

Key Components of Peace with Money

There are certain components of financial peace I've observed that have led to peace with money for my colleagues, clients, friends, and family. These components include the following:

- Being clear about what you want with money, your values, and your actions with money.

- The ability to pay bills, either by yourself or with a partner, in a relaxed manner, with clear communication and a sense of ease, even when there is not enough to pay the bills in full.

- Being flexible about how money is obtained and managed. In other words, being willing to consider that there is more than one way to accomplish monetary activities.

- Examining and addressing self-defeating thoughts, opinions, and conclusions about money (i.e., changing what we tell ourselves).

- Choosing behaviors that support peace rather than disrupt it.

- Living a lifestyle that fits within your current monetary resources so there is little or no stress about whether you will have "enough" money.

- Being free to give of your monetary well-being to others by donations, gifts, or philanthropy.

- A general sense of well-being and security when you think about money.

- Living in a manner that embraces, recognizes, and celebrates all the forms of wealth in your life. These areas of wealth include the following:

- ○ Your physical vitality and well-being.
- ○ A fulfilling spiritual life.
- ○ Harmonious relationships with others.
- ○ Creative expression.
- ○ A sense of delight, happiness, or joy in life.
- ○ Enjoyment of the environment you live in (your home and the landscape around it).
- ○ A spacious sense about time, that you are using time as well as money toward fulfilling pursuits, rather than being driven, feeling overwhelmed, or wanting to escape.

It's valuable to become conscious about what peace with money might look like for you. This picture can be vastly different from person to person.

Regardless of the degree of wealth you have, peace with money is a way of being and a way of feeling that can be cultivated. There are people who choose to manage a monetary lifestyle that includes a seven-thousand-square-foot home on Long Island, a nanny, a housekeeper, a cook, a grounds-keeping crew, a driver, three luxury vehicles, a yacht and crew, and more—at a cost of well over $8 million a year. Yet, without having a feeling of ease and security around money, this lifestyle, for all its magnificence, will bring disharmony and struggle.

Of course, the opposite can be true. If they so choose, the same people could experience their materially abundant lifestyle with a great deal of ease, happiness, and gratitude. The way this lifestyle is perceived depends entirely on the beliefs, perspectives, thinking, and behaviors of those living it. Monetary peace can be as varied as the humans experiencing it.

Peace with money is best expressed through living joyfully with a sense of serenity and harmony. I know a woman whose only possessions are a several-year-old Subaru wagon, a cat, and the belongings that fit into that vehicle. She writes political copy for activist causes and moves about from place to place, providing house- and pet-sitting services for people who are away from their homes for extended periods. Her monetary income averages just $500 to $600 each month, yet she is one of the happiest, most peaceful people I know. She regularly saves 15 percent of her monetary income and contributes 10 percent to causes she believes in. She says the only time she ever experiences disharmony about money is if her cat needs veterinary care or her car needs an unexpected repair and she doesn't have enough in her savings to pay the full amount.

As this woman and I worked together in a coaching relationship, we found that from time to time she has serendipitous inflows of cash. To expand her peace with money, she has chosen to put 30 percent of those "unexpected good" dollars into a cash stash to take care of her cat and car and holds that fund sacred for those two purposes.

For most of us, the amount we live on lies somewhere between these extremes. Yet how many of us can honestly say we are at peace with money most of the time?

Look Money in the Face

Actually staring money "in the face" and observing its effects with clarity and truth can be challenging. Some say doing so feels like one of the most difficult things they could imagine. So they don't think about it. Or at least, they try not to. In actuality, trying not to think about money takes a lot of effort. In most societies, money permeates every activity. Trying not to think about it is rather like the elephant in the room. You want to step around it, but you can't avoid it—especially when a big money mess happens and you have to clean it up. Peace with money? Harmony? Hardly.

Actually thinking through the consequences before putting $6,000 for that all-terrain vehicle on a credit card or spending $300 for new stylish boots is something far too many people have difficulty doing. Never mind the interest rate on the credit card is 19.5 percent. Never mind the toddler is growing out of his clothes and needs new togs. Or that the rent or house payment is due. Better to simply splurge and take the consequences later.

You may not ever do the things with your money that I just mentioned. However, most of us have some form of money madness that exasperates those around us. Without a conscious vision for your money, it becomes far too easy to lose mindfulness and descend into a war with yourself and, by association, others around you. The following exercises will guide you in shifting your money relationship from one of discord to one of peace, greater ease, and, in time, plenitude.

Finding Meaning: Assessing Your Values and Purpose

Our conflicts with ourselves and others often begin when we are not living according to our values, or as my mentor, Maria Nemeth, characterizes them, our "standards of integrity."[11] Some outcomes of the incoherence that arise when we don't live by our values include a general lack of well-being, scarcity, feeling

---

11   Maria Nemeth, *The Energy of Money: A Spiritual Guide to Financial and Personal Fulfillment* (New York: Ballantine, 1997), 65.

cranky with ourselves and others, and taking actions that are outside the bounds of our values.

I encourage you to go to the *Make Peace with Money Workbook*, listed in the resources that follow, and do the Finding Meaning: Assessing Your Values and Purpose exercise found in Lesson 2.

Peace with Money Activities

Write down three situations where you experience conflict about money. If you struggle with money in any way, list it. Your list can be as simple as:

- "I eat out too often."
- "I buy clothes I don't need."
- "I buy specialty coffees every day."
- "I don't pay my bills on time."

Or the list could be more detailed, showing how you feel and what drives you about it:

- "I eat out *X* number of times per month and feel guilty and anxious, but I can't seem to avoid doing it."
- "I buy clothes I don't need, especially boots and purses. I'm ashamed and try to hide my purchases from my spouse."
- "I don't pay my bills on time and often have to pay late fees, putting me in an even tighter financial situation. I get scared and want to ignore the whole thing."

Choose one of the three situations you wrote down and take one small step to begin shifting from struggle to peace. For your first situation, choose one that is yours alone and not something you share with another person. (I encourage you to practice shifting

on your own first without having to address the input of others.)
Answer the following questions:

- Are you willing to own that this situation is yours alone?
- Are you willing to allow some compassion for yourself as you look at this situation?
- What is one small step you can take today to address this situation?

What would peace with money be like for you? Write out what it would look and feel like. When you clearly identify your desires around financial peace, you can begin to make better choices with money and live in more peace with it today.

Bonus Activity: Examine the components of wealth listed earlier in this chapter. Which do you have experience with? Make note of these. Are there forms of wealth you've experienced that are not listed? Add those to your notes. When we recognize and acknowledge the areas in which we experience wealth, we can celebrate it with gratitude. An added benefit is that by experiencing all the ways we are wealthy and feeling grateful rather than burdened, we begin to think more clearly and make better choices with our money. Often we experience more wealth as a result.

Additional Resources

- Refer to the free *Make Peace with Money Workbook* at www.makepeacewithmoney.com, Lesson 2. Log in with the username *makepeacewithmoney* and the password *peace42.*

Chapter 3
DISARMING THE WAR WITH MONEY

Ignoring a bad financial situation is like ignoring your lawn—not paying attention to your grass doesn't mean it stops growing. The longer you don't mow, the harder it is to manage when you finally get the mower out and the more time and work it will take to get the lawn looking good again.

—Shannon Plate

We simply cannot make healthy choices consistently with money while we are in conflict about it. When we don't feel relaxed or at peace with it, we are often in a state of angst, fear, or anger that can border on desperation. We react to financial situations from those states of mind rather than through conscious, intentional choices. We become disconnected from our natural wisdom when we are afraid or angry and it is difficult to find clarity about our financial status when we are caught up in those feelings.

This is not to say you will never make good choices. Actually, many people manage their money reasonably well, regardless of whether they are feeling troubled or peaceful. Making reasonable financial choices just takes a lot more energy when we are at war with money. Therefore, we're likely to make mistakes when we are conflicted about money.

Building a solid foundation of financial harmony frees you up to make wiser choices. With greater clarity, you'll consistently support those choices with appropriate actions. This leads to greater ease with money and an overall happiness and joy that would not be possible otherwise.

This book focuses on six key choices you can make with money that lead to increased well-being. Having been a financial coach for many years, I've observed that when my clients address these choices, they are likely to have a stronger, happier relationship with money, themselves, and others. These six choices are foundational to a harmonious, peace-filled relationship with money. Most importantly, these are choices you can begin implementing now.

Following is a brief overview of the six money-wise choices we'll explore in-depth in subsequent chapters.

1. Choose to Be Conscious about Money

Choosing to be conscious about your money is crucial. Those who go through life on financial autopilot are not likely to be happy about how their money serves them, because they don't actually know how (or even whether) it *is* serving them. In essence, they are enslaved by money because they are constantly unsure about where they stand with it.

When beginning this journey toward peace with money, it's useful to take practical steps right away. Pay unpaid bills or make payment arrangements on past-due bills. Begin shifting your consciousness with money *now*. This is a crucial foundation to all the other changes you'll make.

Money is a form of energy. When we constantly feel as though we are at the mercy of money or are driven by it, our life's energy drains away. We don't enjoy life to its fullest. When we struggle with money, we don't realize the potential energy we can gain when we use our money wisely—money needs clarity and positive action to stay flowing.

Shifting your mind-set to a more positive financial flow means encouraging yourself to be less emotional about it and more matter-of-fact. When you struggle less, you are much more likely to sustain the other steps required to shift your relationship with money. Having a mind-set conducive to monetary peace lays the groundwork for all the steps to come.

The first money-wise choice is to become fully clear about your financial situation without judgmental. You are where you are. In *The Science of Getting Rich*, Wallace Wattles writes, "There is never any time but now, and there never will be any time but now. If you are ever to begin to make ready for the reception of what you want, you must begin now."[12]

You can spurn the effort to become fully conscious about money or you can choose to embrace it. When you embrace it, you open the door to gaining greater certainty. When you begin to see your financial situation with awareness and clear open eyes, you will see where you've been blind, where you've been lying to yourself, and where you've felt like a victim or out of control. You can identify ways to align your money with your goals. You'll begin creating the life you want.

Becoming conscious about finances also means appreciating the fact that money ebbs and flows, so it is unlikely you'll ever gain *complete* control. It's much more effective to learn to have a

12   Wallace Wattles, *The Science of Getting Rich* (n.p.: First Start Publishing e-edition, 2012), 54.

resilient attitude toward money. My own life has been a wild ride of ups and downs with money: unexpected illnesses, the death of a spouse, being hired, being laid off, investments gone bad, investments made good, and so much more. It's only in recent years that my finances have settled into a consistently positive flow. Chances are that you know a number of other people with similar experiences. Perhaps you are one of them.

We can either face challenges feeling defeated from the outset, or we can cultivate resilience and recognize that very few problems are completely insurmountable. Becoming conscious about your finances and embracing flexibility helps foster resilience.

2. Develop a Positive, Affirming Relationship with Money

The next money-wise choice is to develop a positive and affirming relationship with money. You'll assess your beliefs and opinions about money. You'll examine counterproductive stories you tell yourself. This money-wise choice guides you to change your focus toward an abundance mind-set (a mind-set that values positivity, wisdom, and responsibility).

Once you begin changing old beliefs to more empowering ones, you'll feel yourself lightening up. Changing how you think about money might seem a little strange at the start. You may not believe you can do it. Training your mind is, in essence, similar to training your body. You work out at the gym and at first it seems difficult. You may even feel awkward when you get on a treadmill or stationary bike. Yet, if you keep at it, your strength, balance, and stamina increase. The same thing happens on a mental and emotional level when you do the exercises in this book and the companion workbook. As you consciously attend to your thoughts about money, they will shift toward greater peace.

3. Determine Your Money's Purpose

It's essential to determine the purpose you want money to serve. This is your foundation for a happier relationship with money. Do you want your personal time and energy to be spent primarily earning money? Or do you prefer to live so that your money serves your life's purpose and areas that support it?

As a coach, I work with people to determine what they truly desire for their lives. When you connect your life's intentions to your money, you'll see how it can serve a positive function beyond simply paying bills. When money serves your purposes, taking good care of your money becomes less stressful. Having a vision or purpose for your money helps you stay on track with your big-picture goals.

Conversely, knowing your goals can help you stay on track with money. It becomes a positive feedback loop rather than the negative thought patterns we humans often fall into. When your life's intentions and use of money are aligned, you are more likely to be clear about how you want your money to be used to fulfill those intentions.

4. Determine How You Most Want Money to Serve You

We all play games with money. Usually, we either feel like a winner or a loser with it. We win some and we lose some, just as we do when playing sports or a computer game. The difference in sports and computer games is that typically we learn the rules, then hone our skills with practice in order to master the game. Yet have we put the same attention and effort to learning mastery with money? Some people do, and if you are one who has done so, congratulations.

Many more of us slide by, learning just enough to keep us from getting into trouble. Or, in some cases, just enough to get us into deep trouble: the deep water of debt and disgruntlement about money.

When you choose to become as competent with your use of money as you are skilled in other areas of your life, you'll find that your money begins to serve you.

How have you played the game so far? Are you just barely making it financially? Do you have enough, but are spending in ways that don't provide you with deep satisfaction? Do you feel like you are drowning in debt? Do you want more money? If so, how much more? Or do you want to be happier and more effective with the money you already have?

In this step, you begin to build your money vision. How do you most want your money to serve you? Your vision for your money can be virtually anything. In fact, I encourage you to dream boldly. As you dream, keep sight of the intentions you have for your life. When we get excited about possibilities for our lives, we generate an energy that is conducive to taking positive actions with our money.

Setting up your vision, coherent with the purpose you've identified, can bring you hope and anticipation. Both emotions help keep you motivated to take authentic actions—those actions that propel you toward a more fulfilling life overall and direct your use of money to serve your vision.

5. Take Care of Details

Taking care of details means knowing exactly where you stand financially: what you owe and what you own. In this section, you'll learn precisely how much income you have, from what sources, and how much your expenses are. You'll discover your net worth, and you'll see why keeping your bank account balanced is valuable to fulfilling your purpose and vision.

Attending to your financial details keeps your situation real rather than nebulous. When you know where you stand, you can use that knowledge as the foundation to build a better monetary scenario for yourself. Attending to details lets you consciously build the life you truly desire rather than having a "someday" dream.

The more willing you are to address the details of your financial life, the easier it is to learn your numbers with clarity and accuracy.

Many people have little idea what they actually spend or what they need to spend daily, weekly, monthly, or annually. They don't budget, plan, and save for annual expenses (such as taxes or auto, health, and home insurance). They don't plan for and save for emergencies. This creates unnecessary stress when surprise expenses come up, such as a dental work or new tires costing $500 to $1,000 or more.

As you keep track of your money day-to-day, you'll become clear about what you actually need to spend. You'll distinguish between the things you merely want and those required to fulfill actual needs such as food, shelter, transportation, and utilities.

You will establish systems for tracking income and expenses and get into the habit of tracking every place you spend money.

Jennifer felt terrible every time she had to take care of bills. She made frequent errors, resulting in overdraft fees that amounted to hundreds of dollars over the course of a year. Her errors resulted in feelings of guilt, helplessness, and stupidity.

Using the Make Peace with Money program, she developed a more positive relationship with money and began to love knowing her numbers. She monitored her income and tracked expenses daily. She was no longer fearful to do her banking and found that, by delighting in knowing where she stood, she was getting even better numbers.

You don't need to be a financial wizard to get good at details. With the information in this book, you'll learn to look objectively at your financial situation. Knowing your numbers and revising your mind-set is of enormous help in generating peace with money.

If you tend to be more of an artistic big-picture person who focuses on creativity and finds these financial details boring or overwhelming, I encourage you to ask for some help. If you can afford it, hire a bookkeeper. They can keep track of the details for you, although, I encourage you to review your books once a month to stay in touch with your financial picture.

If money is a concern, a number of free and low-cost apps exist that make tracking spending, saving, and investing much easier than it has ever been. If you are unfamiliar with how to use apps for your phone or computer, there are classes at community colleges, universities, small business–development centers, and senior centers that can help you learn how to use them. You can also ask someone who is between the ages of eighteen and thirty-five what they use—chances are good they will have a recommendation.

Though it will take some time and focus to learn about this, I assure you that once you have, you'll find tracking your financial situation will become much simpler.

6. Don't Do It Alone

Even if you consider yourself to be highly self-sufficient, it can be enormously valuable to have the support of people you can count on to provide sound information—mentors to learn from, and people who can help as you question your beliefs and habits with money. This decision to accept and receive the support of others is one of the smartest decisions you can make in regard to money.

While you'll learn more about getting support in a subsequent chapter, I cannot emphasize this basic principle enough: get support. Support can come in many forms. You might opt for financial coaching with someone who works with clients the way I do. You may hire an accountant or bookkeeper. Some people find excellent investment advisers. Others create a small group of friends who support one another in getting out of debt or share strategies to grow their incomes. There are as many options as there are unique individuals in the world, but the point is, don't isolate yourself. Who you choose for support depends, in part, on your particular needs.

It is strange how we are so thoroughly immersed in a money-based system and yet it is so taboo to discuss our money with others. So we don't discuss it, or talk in generalities. We often feel isolated or don't have current, useful information that could help us. I encourage you to seek the help of professionals or knowledgeable acquaintances. Know that you don't have to struggle with money alone. We'll delve into how you can build a support system that works for you in a subsequent chapter.

You will see by the progression of these money-wise choices that it all begins with the mind-set we bring to our circumstances. Financial experts will counsel you to first stop creating more debt immediately. This is certainly wise. But without a shift in thinking and behavior, you may get out of debt, only to fall right back into it, why? Because your self-defeating thoughts and actions have not been addressed. We must address the root cause.

As you work with the accompanying workbook, take the time to lay a new, strong foundation for yourself through changing how you think about and behave with money. Examine your beliefs. Discover what conclusions you automatically leap to and determine whether those conclusions serve or undermine what you desire most.

By the time you reach the practical strategies found in the later chapters, you will be ready (even eager) to engage in the tips, exercises, and approaches I suggest to empower your relationship with money and, ultimately, make peace with it.

Peace with Money Activities

Your money autobiography

Write a one- to two-page money biography. When you do so, look especially at your thinking patterns, the choices you make, and habits you've fallen into. You likely will discover some thoughts or beliefs you have taken on from others, be it your parents, your peers, or your community. Use these questions to guide your discovery about yourself:

- What is your earliest memory about money?

- What attitudes about or habits with money did the adults in your life demonstrate?

- What attitudes or habits did you take on as a result of witnessing those of the adults in your life?

- What do you say about money when you have it? When you don't have it?

- How do you feel about money now?

- What have you done with money that was most challenging to you?

- What have you done with money that has delighted you?

- What or who in your adult life has influenced your thinking or behaviors regarding money?

- What is a significant failure you've had with money? What is a significant success?

Additional Resources

- Refer to the free *Make Peace with Money Workbook* at www.makepeacewithmoney.com, Lesson 3. Log in with the username *makepeacewithmoney* and the password *peace42*.

- *The Energy of Money: A Spiritual Guide to Financial and Personal Fulfillment* by Maria Nemeth.

- YNAB (free downloadable software): www.youneedabudget. com

Chapter 4
BECOMING CONSCIOUS ABOUT YOUR MONEY

How can one be a wise man, if he does not know any better how to live than other men?

—Henry David Thoreau

To make a lasting change, you must become conscious of how you relate to money and how it affects you—even as you begin taking practical steps to change your financial behavior. Too many of us hope that money will bring happiness. The truth is that happiness is an inside job, not dependent on others or objects but only ourselves.

You may think, "Once I have this or that material thing, or the perfect relationship, or a fabulous job, or more money, then I'll be happy." The truth is that things bought with money can bring temporary pleasure or satisfaction. Yet they rarely, if ever, bring true happiness.

Psychologist and author Margaret Paul says, "Happiness is not something that happens to you. It is something you choose or don't choose each and every moment."[13]

<u>Become aware</u> of what you think is causing your happiness.

13 Margaret Paul, "Happiness Is an Inside Job," *HuffPost*, last updated April 26, 2015, https://www.huffingtonpost.com/margaret-paul-phd/happiness-is-an-inside-jo_1_b_6734960.html.

Notice whether your focus is on external circumstances or things to "make" you happy. When you look inside yourself, you may realize you have a lot to be grateful for. You may naturally begin to seek the joy of giving to others. You may find yourself seeking to experience a quiet happiness in each moment.

Becoming conscious means attending to your thoughts and feelings throughout the day. Choose thoughts that support your aims rather than those that undermine your efforts. Make money choices aligned with the life you envision. Be fully aware of how you receive and spend your money. Consciousness includes tuning in to the emotions you have about money. Letting emotions drive you can lead to behavior that undermines your life vision.

Many of us go through life without making an effort to unearth that which causes stress or leaves us filled with fear and dread whenever we think about money. We tend to think pained emotions around money are natural and cannot be changed.

The truth is these beliefs and emotions *can* be changed. The evidence is found among the hundreds of people I've coached who gained a different perspective on their money and changed their behavior accordingly.

Money and Your Relationship with Yourself

An excellent starting point for consciousness with money is to notice its impact on your relationships. Our relationships reveal a great deal about us if we are willing to look. How you behave with money in your relationship with yourself, your partner, your family, your bank, even with money itself—all of these serve as powerful reflective tools to grow your awareness of how money influences you.

Have you ever found yourself fighting with yourself about how you spend your money? Do you berate yourself for not making enough money? What about your partner or other family members? Have you found that talking about money with your partner or family sometimes ends in an argument or bad feelings?

Fighting with yourself about money can undermine your self-confidence and deplete energy you could be using to accomplish the dreams and goals you have for yourself and those you treasure.

Here are some ways to tell if you are fighting with yourself about money:

- You go shopping and spontaneously buy something. You know you should put off buying it until you have the cash in hand or the money in the bank, but you charge it instead. And then you beat yourself up all the way home for having bought it.

- You feel trapped in a job that pays significantly less than you are worth, yet you're scared to ask for a raise.

- Perhaps you need to spend money on something necessary, like dental work, but instead you spend it going on an adventure with friends. Meanwhile, your teeth are causing you pain.

- You sometimes hold back from spending on something you need, such as new tires for your car or shoes for your child, for no particular reason. Yet your tires are getting balder and the shoes are pinching his feet. This kind of withholding can ultimately cost more than the savings should you have an accident or the child need orthotics.

Look clearly to identify where you leak or withhold money.

Addressing what you discover opens the door to greater peace in your personal relationship with it.

Money and Your Relationships with Others

Often the war we wage with ourselves around money leaks into our interactions with others. We project our angst onto those around us and take on an attitude of "they're out to get me." For example, say your high-interest credit cards tacked on an "account balance protection" charge. Rather than negotiating with the creditors to have the extra charges removed, you characterize them as heartless money machines who wouldn't listen to you even if you called.

This is fear-based thinking, giving your power over to the impersonal. Ultimately, you disempower yourself when you think this way. This mind-set is full of self-limiting internal chatter. If you don't allow yourself to be driven by that chatter and take a positive action instead, you choose your well-being over fear or mistrust.

Fear and mistrust have even worse results when we take our money war into our relationships with loved ones. The money-and-relationships mixture is so volcanic that innumerable books have been written about it. It would be wise for new lovers of any age to understand how vital it is to marry someone who is on a similar financial wavelength.

If your partner's thinking and behavior with money is significantly different from yours, if you seek to have harmony in your relationship with money, talk about those differences and make clear agreements. When couples (or even roommates) make this effort, they are much less likely to fight about money from the beginning.

If you are already in a relationship, you can still come to an agreement, so you can stop fighting and handle monetary situations better. This takes maturity and emotional intelligence on the part of each partner. If discord about money has been a consistent aspect of your relationship, I encourage you to get some assistance by working with a coach or counselor to work through your differences and make agreements about how the two of you intend to proceed.

Here are examples of couples with very different approaches to handling money. Imagine a financially responsible woman, one who tracks every single expense, marrying a financially carefree man. (Of course, the opposite scenario is also a reality, with the man being fiscally aware and the woman more unconcerned. Note that this applies to alternatively gendered relationships as well.) He rarely knows how much he has in his account to spend on necessities, much less the finer things of life, but he would much rather play with money than attend to details.

The partners might be crazy in love, but over time, the impractical reality of being polar opposites when it comes to handling money will create a strain in their relationship unless they resolve it early on.

Money is usually not discussed in much detail by couples in the early stages of a relationship. As soon as partners get seriously involved, however, finances become a vital element to be addressed sooner rather than later, in order to have a harmonious relationship. Staying conscious and noticing how the other person handles money can give you clues even when you aren't yet ready to overtly discuss money.

When you feel despair about money, chances are your partner, parents, or children are affected. Conversely, when others who are close to you feel challenged with money, you will feel it too. From my own experience, I've learned some tough yet worthwhile lessons, thanks to relationships I've had with differing approaches to money.

Here's an example from my own life. My husband and I have worked out a system where we address our finances and pay bills twice each month—together. Believe me, this is an ongoing exercise in staying conscious to my desire to have peace in every area of my life. Specifically, I must stay conscious of my desire for peace with money when we're paying bills, and I must focus on my intention to love and appreciate my husband.

My husband and I are as different as an abacus and a smartphone in our approach to almost everything we do. So, naturally, each of us thinks and acts differently with money. We've been married more than twenty years, and it's taken a lot of experimentation and intentional communication to get where we are now.

A resource that helped us learn to communicate more effectively, especially about money, is Marshall Rosenberg's book *Nonviolent Communication*. We learned to get in touch with our feelings and needs to communicate in a way that does not make the other person "wrong." This style of communication has been so powerful in helping us reach accord on money issues. These days, we are almost always harmonious when paying our bills.

My husband and I have to be willing to listen to each other's point of view and be flexible (even when I'm quite sure my way is "right"). I must remember that peace in every area of my life is far more important to me than "being right." And I have to remain clear that I love him so much more than I do my own opinions, beliefs, and conclusions about how money "should" be handled. Over the years, maintaining a peaceful relationship where money is concerned has also required quite a few apologies from each of us for terse words or a sharp tone of voice.

Through my second and third marriages, as well as the early years of my current marriage, I intentionally kept my finances separate from my spouse's. In my first marriage, my husband and I combined our funds in a single bank account, and our interactions in regard to money were nearly always volatile. Keeping my money separate was in the interest of not fighting about money. I'd experienced enough acrimony surrounding finances in my parents' household and during my first marriage—I was determined not to let money be the cause of more conflict.

Notice that my behavior was in the interest of *not fighting about* money rather than in the interest of *achieving peace with* money. At that time, the concept of peace with money was so invisible to me I couldn't even have had that thought. It has only been during the past decade that I've actively sought peace with money rather than seeking to not fight about it.

My other partners were in agreement that it was best to keep our finances separately. For six months of the year, I'd write a check to my partner for my share of our joint expenses and he'd pay the bills. The other six months of the year, I'd pay the bills and he'd write a check to me.

That system meant we didn't know very much about what our partner spent money on. Or whether either of us had any sort of savings. Each of us contributed $50 a month to a joint savings account that was supposed to be set aside for a vacation or some other special event. But it almost always got spent to replace the car tires, pay for a chiropractic adjustment, or some other "emergency." If we had a sudden need, such as an auto repair or a trip to deal with an elderly parent's problems, there was always discord. If one person seemed to have plenty while the other was struggling to have enough, that contributed to conflict as well.

My partners and I rarely earned similar amounts. Significant discord occurred when one of us spent money on an extravagance without consulting the other, even though we had agreed to keep our funds separate.

It quickly became clear that I thought the new power drill he purchased for several hundred dollars was a luxury while he "knew" it was a necessity. And the new little black dress with business jacket, scarves, jewelry, and pumps I purchased—so I could go from daytime business to evening chic without changing clothes—seemed wholly unnecessary to him, while to me it felt like a "business essential."

When it came time to do joint taxes, the stress in the household was palpable for several days until the taxes were done. All this in the interest of not fighting about money.

While my current husband and I have definitely been annoyed with each other at times over how we spent our money, we are fortunate to have enough money to meet our needs.

Some people are in relationships where there is simply not enough to pay the bills. This can lead to an overarching feeling of despair about money and, thus, strife within the relationship. If you are in a relationship like this, it is vital you begin taking steps to address and reduce your own feeling of despair. You don't even have to be stone broke to feel despair; plenty of people who are financially well-off get caught up in that feeling of "not enough."

In later chapters I share ways to alleviate the despair. However, when it comes to being conscious, for now, just let yourself become aware of the emotions you feel. Write them down and seek to be aware of how they affect your relationships.

Simply realizing how your actions and emotions impact you and others can show you what to focus on first to begin shifting your situation. As you gain awareness, you can define intentions, then small actions and even larger goals, for yourself, or within your partnership.

The Copycat Effect: How You Behave with Money Affects Your Children

If you have children, your relationship with money affects them. Here are some questions to ask yourself to discover how you might be influencing them:

- Are you conscious about what you share with them about money?
- Beyond what you tell them, how do they see you act with money?
- What kind of role models did you have growing up?
- Are you repeating patterns your parents displayed? Or are you creating new ones?
- Are you setting your children up for success with money, or are they destined to repeat your patterns?

Children are easily influenced by attitudes and behavior. The next generation in your family will have a greater likelihood of peace with their money when you come to peace with it yourself.

A Coaching Story: Matthew's Money Journey

Working as a financial coach for many years, I have numerous examples of how beneficial financial coaching can be. One of my favorites is the story of Matthew, a young man who was motivated to make a difference in the world. He gave me permission to tell his inspiring story which I'll weave throughout the remaining chapters.

Matthew came to me seeking help to determine how he could pay off his considerable college debt. By the time I met him, Matthew was a kind and responsible young man with a huge heart. There had been a point, however, when Matthew was severely off-track. As we began working together, we uncovered his war with money.

At age fifteen, Matthew ran away from an abusive home. Until that time, he rarely handled money other than his allowance and small amounts he earned from summer lawn care jobs. He ended up living on the streets of a large city in the Southwest. There, he connected with street folk who convinced him that money was no good—money was not to be trusted and it was better to get whatever he needed for free.

The suspicious yet entitled attitude of these people influenced Matthew's thinking, and he learned to disdain money. So much so that whenever he received some from odd jobs or, more often, from selling his body, he gave it away or spent it on marijuana or cheap sherry. Because he'd had no guidance from his family about money before he ran away, he was unable to understand how his money might better be used to care for himself to buy food, transportation to a job, or even a residence.

A kind man employed by the homeless shelter in the city began to talk with Matthew whenever the teenager showed up there.

Matthew listened. He started changing his life, little by little. He began by doing some janitorial work for the shelter. Eventually, he stopped living on the streets and returned to high school, where he did well. However, the echoes of those early street lessons about money lingered.

By the time Matthew started college to become a social worker like the man who had helped him, he was substantially conflicted about spending the money required to get his degree. He felt he was acting responsibly by going to college, yet as a result of the "training" he received from the street people, he also felt entitled to the educational loans. He didn't spend his money well.

The amount of debt he accrued was compounded by the ease with which he was able to obtain loans. Like many in college, he got his first credit card, and then several more. Matthew originally hoped his graduation day would be filled with joy, but he graduated with more than $72,000 in debt. He felt powerless and trapped, not at all sure how he would pay such a massive sum on a social worker's salary.

"I'm so stupid," he said. "How did I ever let myself get into this situation?"

The first thing I asked Matthew to do was get completely clear about the truth of his financial situation. Step-by-step, we chipped away at what he didn't know. It was clear Matthew wasn't stupid. He was simply ignorant of the information he needed to be successful with his money.

If you'll recall, the definition of success with money is doing what you say you will do with it, consistently and with clarity, focus, ease, and grace. Once Matthew gained awareness about his situation, he began to see on his own what his next steps would be, both to address his current situation and to plan for a better financial future.

I will refer to Matthew throughout the next chapters, as his is a story that effectively illustrates the usefulness of money-wise choices. By the end of chapter 12, you will see through Matthew's story how one person applied these concepts in a practical manner to his great benefit.

You can find peace and harmony with money—peace with yourself and in your relationships with others—even in circumstances as dramatic as Matthew's.

The first step is to consciously choose that you want more peace and harmony. Get a clear image of how you want to be with money. Once you see how you want your life and money to be, you'll practice what it takes to get there. For me and many of my clients, it's taken a good deal of practice. I can guarantee the effort is worth it. To have peace of mind is so deeply satisfying.

Peace with Money Activities

Now that you've done your money biography from chapter 3, let's look at your current situation. Write down your answers to the questions that follow. When you only think about the concepts, you are less likely to take the steps required to rectify the situation.

- When you experience a sense of rightness about money, what is going on? What is one small step you can take this week to build on this?
- Are you in conflict with yourself about money? In what way?
- Are you in conflict with others about money? In what way?

- What do you earn? Does it meet your financial requirements? Is it enough? Is it more than enough?

- How about your expenses? Are they regularly more than your income? Or do you keep them less than your income, but then at times feel deprived?

- Do you ever spend money on things that don't satisfy you or that you don't need?

- Do you have debt (credit card balances, auto loans, college loans, and so on)? Do you know exactly what you owe?

- What small step could you take today to resolve the debt you are currently carrying?

- What can you do this week (or even today) to improve your financial situation?

- Who do you know that can support you in making the changes you wish to make?

Additional Resources

- Refer to the free *Make Peace with Money Workbook* at www.makepeacewithmoney.com, Lesson 4. Log in with the username *makepeacewithmoney* and the password *peace42*.

- *The Soul of Money: Transforming Your Relationship with Money and Life* by Lynne Twist.

- *Couples Money: What Every Couple Should Know about Money and Relationships* by Marlow Felton and Chris Felton.

- *Financial Recovery: Developing a Healthy Relationship with Money* by Karen McCall.

- *The Energy of Money: A Spiritual Guide to Financial and Personal Fulfillment* by Maria Nemeth.

- *Money Harmony: A Road Map for Individuals and Couples* by Olivia Mellan and Sherry Christie.

Chapter 5

BUILDING A POSITIVE RELATIONSHIP WITH MONEY

When we do what we are meant to do, money comes to us, doors open for us, we feel useful, and the work we do feels like play to us.

—Julia Cameron

Developing an active, affirmative relationship with money is a crucial choice. Why is this kind of relationship so valuable?

What we think and believe can become reality. Countless books, essays, movies, and self-development programs revolve around this concept. While the term "law of attraction" has gained a great deal of attention in recent years, the concepts are not new at all. Writers such as Wallace Wattles, Napoleon Hill, and U. S. Andersen were all proponents of this concept during the early part of the twentieth century. The law of attraction is the belief that by focusing on positive or negative thoughts a person brings positive or negative experiences into their life.

The core of this concept is for you to observe your thoughts. Is what you are thinking framed in positive terms? Or in negative terms? If you are unsure, check in with how you feel about the thought. Do you feel positive and energized? Or is your energy low? Are you feeling sad or depressed or some other negative feeling? You might consider keeping a thought journal to record your thoughts. Make note of whether they seem positive or negative to you. When you write them down, it's easier to see how you want to reframe them either to come from negative to positive or from somewhat positive to even more positive. When I worry about something, my energy goes down and I'm less able to make positive choices.

I invite you to pay close attention to your thoughts and deliberately choose the ones that serve you well rather than those that do not. In turn, you can create a positive situation around you when you take actions that are aligned with effective thoughts. When you do this, your thoughts and actions are more likely to serve you well.

Those actions that are aligned with and support your desired thoughts, goals, and dreams are called authentic actions. Discern the difference between authentic actions and habitual actions. Some habitual actions are driven by old beliefs and keep you going around in circles with little or no positive results. When you identify those, stop doing them and turn your actions and energy toward what you want. In addition, note those actions that address the tasks of your life (such as organizing your data files or cleaning the garage) that are valuable yet don't advance your vision for your life and money. I encourage you to take care of this kind of task as efficiently as possible, to free your energy.

Even when we practice choosing more effective thoughts and act to bring those thoughts into the reality we desire, life will inevitably present us with challenges. Entertaining only positive thoughts does not mean your life becomes perfect. Instead, by expanding your thinking to invite a broader variety of responses and more flexibility, you'll develop greater resilience and respond to the difficulties life hands you in a healthier way. This makes a significant difference to the level of peace you can experience, even in the face of those difficulties. You'll be able to handle the ups and downs life presents you with greater clarity, agility, and compassion toward yourself and others.

Not long ago, a situation stretched me beyond what I could have imagined. My ninety-one-year-old mother-in-law had a series of severe strokes. A delightful and charming woman throughout her later years, after the strokes she became terrified, temperamental, and filled with anger. She lashed out at those around her and talked incoherently and erratically. She had no sense whatsoever of what was safe or unsafe and could have easily walked out in front of a car had we not watched her closely. She needed to use a walker but could not remember to do so. She had to be supervised 24-7 and each day a great many decisions had to be made about her care.

Mom lived a nine-hour drive from my home. It was unfeasible for my husband to leave his work to help. Because my work was flexible, and because I loved her dearly, I was able to step in to support my sister-in-law, who lived with Mom and who, even though she was a trained nurse, felt overwhelmed with the depth of care her mother required. Once I arrived, it became clear that both of us needed to focus solely on Mom's care and that I must not try to pursue work as I'd intended. This meant I would forego my business income for an indeterminate amount of time. Nevertheless, I was willing.

A month after the strokes occurred, my mother-in-law died. Three days later, I became seriously ill. The amount of income-making work I could do was severely limited for several more months. To say that all of this was both emotionally and financially challenging is an understatement. Yet, by and large, I was able to hold on to a sense of peace and equanimity during those long months.

You may ask, "How did you do it?"

I began by acknowledging that peace, even in severe circumstances, is possible. Nelson Mandela is one of my inspirations, as are Anne Frank and Viktor Frankl. Each rose above seemingly insurmountable obstacles—much more difficult than the ones I'd had to face—to inspire others with their light. I told myself that if Mandela could go through prison and come out the leader he was, then surely I could weather what I was experiencing.

This is one of the secrets to peace: taking inspiration from those who've gone before.

Another crucial step, whether you are building a positive relationship with money or choosing a peaceful state of mind, is to stay present and focused on dealing with each challenge that may arise—while letting go of concerns about the past or the future. I found I was able to do this by using a brief contemplation I'd learned a couple of years earlier. It involved breathing deeply into the belly and then on the exhale stating, "May I be happy." Inhale, exhale, "May I be peaceful." Inhale, exhale, "May all beings be happy." Inhale, exhale, "May all beings be peaceful." Repeat this as often as needed to bring forth a sense of calm.

The recitation of, "May I be peaceful, may all beings be peaceful," was especially valuable for me in that I needed to keep my distance from others during my illness as my own immune system was quite vulnerable. Those words reminded me that I still had a place in the larger scheme of life.

This method of calling forth peace might or might not work for you. For some, prayer is most effective; for others, meditation. Journaling is also helpful. What is important is that you seek to discover what brings peace to *you*, even when you're in turmoil, and then make a practice of intentionally invoking peace into all aspects of your life—including money.

The possible effects of observing and changing your thought patterns about money can be profound. Where money is concerned, it can be quite obvious (to others, though not necessarily to you) when your limiting beliefs are holding you back. It is as if you are dancing with a partner who has limited steps and no desire whatsoever to improve their dancing skills. You would be unlikely to become a more skillful dancer if you stayed with that partner. Your thoughts are your dance partners. They can either hold you back or move you forward.

Fundamental to making peace with money is discovering your limiting beliefs, then acting to change them. If a certain thought isn't getting you where you want to be, examine it—especially if you notice this is not the first time you've had that thought.

Determine if you are willing to change your limiting thoughts about money. When we choose to give ourselves empowering and loving messages about money (and anything else in our lives), we're much more likely to experience a life that is filled not only with monetary wealth but also a wealth of healthy relationships, greater physical well-being, joy, creativity, and more.

There are as many limiting beliefs about money as there are unique minds believing them. Before we look at a few of the more common beliefs I've observed, I want to demonstrate just how beliefs come to be planted in our minds and put forth the premise that we have the power within us to shift those beliefs.

I want to share a story about a young woman I know who truly transformed a legacy of limited beliefs and created a new standard within her family.

Changing a Legacy of Beliefs

Brandy was fifteen when I met her. She had applied to be a volunteer intern with the public relations department that I led.

Brandy's mother, grandmother, and great-grandmother had relied on public assistance (such as food subsidies, early childhood programs, subsidized housing, Medicaid, disability, and other social services) since well before Brandy's mother was born. While welfare and other support structures provide invaluable assistance to people in genuine need, Brandy's family members had come to believe all this support was their just due; they felt entitled and made little or no effort to gain or hold employment, or to bring in an income through their own initiative. In fact, they did pretty much everything they could to avoid work, including bearing child after child out of wedlock so they could avail themselves of even more support. Brandy had nine aunts and uncles. Most of them received welfare or, in the case of the uncles, were either on disability or producing illicit drugs (or both).

The adults in Brandy's family complained bitterly about how little money they had and how the wealthy of the world owed them a better living. Brandy and her six younger siblings appeared, for all intents and purposes, to be headed down the same path.

This was the only way of life Brandy had ever known. Then something changed. While still an adolescent, Brandy's social studies teacher assigned her students, many of whom were in similar circumstances to Brandy's, to study the value of self-determination to self-esteem. Difficult and abstract concepts, it would seem, for a twelve-year-old. Yet somehow it lit a fire in Brandy. She realized she did not want to continue her family's pattern of entitlement, lack of self-worth, and discord around money.

Brandy asked her teacher how she could go about changing her life and expectations. She read biographies of successful women who began life in difficult circumstances. And the teacher met with her periodically to guide her quest. At her church, at her school, and in the community, she began to watch and listen to people who had money. She avidly scrutinized Oprah Winfrey's life story, realizing that Oprah, too, had come from poverty yet experienced great success.

Brandy learned that many people who had money delighted in being supportive of others in their own communities or beyond. Far from being greedy and domineering (which was her family's characterization of them), the people she studied were almost always generous, kind, and pleasant to be around. While they lived good lives themselves and supported their families well, they also gave to their churches and to causes they believed in; in fact, they often gave to several different organizations.

With the support of her teacher, Brandy set herself on a course to attend college. Having read biographies of poor women who received scholarships to get a higher education, she pursued scholarship support. She studied hard and did well in high school, all the while being taunted by family members for her "uppity ways."

Brandy considered which skills would be useful as an adult and started volunteering where she could obtain and then hone those skills. She was a high school sophomore when we met. At the end of her junior year, she learned that a health organization, where she'd volunteered since she was fourteen, planned to give her a full four-year scholarship to college.

Fast-forward twenty-two years. Brandy is an administrator with a PhD, working at a Midwestern hospital and earning a strong six-figure income. She is married with two adolescent children who volunteer in their community. She passionately contributes both time and money to organizations and causes that help those on public assistance become self-supporting.

Now adults themselves, none of her six younger siblings is receiving public assistance and four have graduated from college. Brandy works hard, and she loves her work. She says it almost doesn't seem like work to her. She has earned the harmony she experiences in her financial and personal life.

Is every moment of Brandy's life filled with peace? Of course not. For example, Brandy was an executive at a hospital that underwent the transition from keeping paper files on patients to digital records. This was chaotic for many employees. Brandy endured many long hours training and intensively supervising during the changeover. She has adolescent children, a husband who is sometimes cranky, aunts and uncles who still chronically complain and deride her, and an aged dog that sometimes poops on the rug. There are moments, sometimes even whole days, when she is not at peace. Yet the arc of her life as a whole is filled with plenty, joy, and, yes, a good deal of peace.

In large measure, Brandy's life is fulfilling because she chose to learn the information needed to build a good relationship with money and have healthy relationships with others in her life. She examined her own beliefs, as well as those of her family. She chose to *think* differently and *act* differently. She found inspiration in the biographies she read and the wealthy people she met, and she asked mentors to guide her. Brandy changed the prevailing familial pattern and limiting belief that the world owed her a living. As a result, Brandy created a vastly different outcome for her life.

The Stumbling Blocks

You can absorb nearly an infinite number of beliefs during your life. Some are beneficial. Some are limiting. Let's take a look at a few that get in the way of a healthy, peace-filled relationship with money.

"I Deserve This"

One example of a limiting belief is an attitude that says, "I deserve this." You may think you deserve to buy something whether or not you actually have the money to purchase it, so you go into debt to get it. If you believe you're entitled to that item, then you'll think more about the object you're buying than you do about the debt you'll incur or what that debt will mean later when the bill comes due.

"I Don't Deserve This"

The flip side of "I deserve this" is "I don't deserve this." This limiting belief can include those things you already have. When you believe you "don't deserve" to have money or other belongings, one result is not earning as much money as your work is worth. You may also give away your money or belongings to fill another's "need" (whether that need is real or is a need you imagine the other person has), so that you don't have to feel guilty because you have more than you deserve.

"I'm Bad with Money"

If you believe "I'm bad with money," as I did for many years, you might feel despairing about your finances. You won't bother to keep good records or plan with much, if any, care. You won't want to see your money details because it can be scary to see how little you have.

Like me, you may tell yourself, "I don't know who to trust." Or you may think, "I don't know what to look for if I ask someone to help me. They'll take advantage or defraud me." Or this might feel familiar: "I'm so bad with money I don't know what to do. I might as well go buy something." This, of course, leads to solidifying your belief about being bad with money.

"If I Don't Have Money, I Won't Become Degraded by It"

Another limiting belief is that money is somehow "dirty" or beneath you—that you'll be tainted if you were to actually have a goodly amount of it. Many Western cultures use the term "filthy lucre." This implies money is procured by ill-conceived or dishonest means. The belief many take on seems to be, "If I don't have money, I won't become degraded by it." So you shortchange yourself by not standing up for yourself when negotiating a salary or hourly wage and are offered less than you are worth based on education or experience.

A parallel belief about money as demeaning is a belief that money is somehow not spiritual or holy. With this kind of thinking, you may denounce money because it is not divine.

The truth is this: money is simply a unit of exchange, an energy that is neither good nor bad. You give money power and meaning, as we all do, by how you think about and behave with it.

You can choose to use your money in ways that bring unholy results, or you can choose to use money in ways that bring about well-being, spiritual good, and benefit for yourself and others.

When you give money, you can give it in a way that can be transformative to both your own and the receiver's lives.

Other Limiting Beliefs

Many other things we say about money get in the way of having a strong relationship with it. Here are a few examples:

- "Money's meant to be spent."
- "It's only money. It's just not that important."
- "There's not enough money to go around."
- "People have to work too hard to get lots of money. I just can't do that."
- "I don't want to work, work, work, and not have a life."

Discovering Limiting Beliefs

One way to discover your self-limiting conversations and become more effective, happier, and more at peace with your money is to make note of your self-talk during the times you're feeling uncomfortable about money. Carry a little notebook or record your thoughts into your smartphone. Capturing limiting thoughts when you have them is a first step toward changing them into more supportive ones.

As humans, we are quick to jump to conclusions about ourselves or others in regard to money. Once we have a conclusion (for example, "I'm bad with money"), we begin gathering evidence to substantiate it. With the evidence in place ("I'm bad with money because my bills are never paid on time"), we behave in a certain way. This could be that we postpone paying bills until some of them are overdue. Then others behave in a certain way; in this instance, by calling us to collect the past-due bills or sending late notices. These actions reinforce the original conclusion that "I'm bad with money." And round and round we go!

When you first discover your limiting beliefs and conclusions, you might decide to seek the help of a coach, therapist, or other professional. The goal is to discover what thoughts are limiting you and replace them with more empowering ones. Others can help you see or hear what you may have become so accustomed to that you wouldn't observe it about yourself.

Limiting thoughts and beliefs get set into our minds from a young age, so it is essential to understand that they are just thoughts. You don't have to let them drive you. You can make your own choices in every moment. You can take control. If you've never before had the conscious thought that you have a choice about what you believe about money, take a moment to try to identify a time when you have chosen one belief over another.

Jerry's Story

Jerry decided when he was quite young that his dad was hopelessly old-fashioned and didn't know anything about money or how to support his kids. After all, his dad made a good wage at the power plant. Why didn't Jerry have all the toys and treats other kids had?

And why was Jerry's dad so set on all his kids going to college? After all, neither of Jerry's parents had a higher education. As the oldest, Jerry was influential in convincing his younger siblings of his conclusion about their dad's financial ineptness. Jerry frequently rebelled and ultimately left home to make his fortune. He decided he wanted to provide more for his children than his father had.

It wasn't until he was out on his own that he fully understood why the family had lived such a modest, even frugal, life rather than the more extravagant life of his friends' families. From the time Jerry was born, his parents saved 25 percent of their income to create college funds for each of their children. The parents were open with their children about the fund, but Jerry had never actually thought about the impact that saving had had on the family.

Jerry realized his characterizations about his dad had no basis. Fortunately, he was big enough to admit he was wrong, not only to his parents but also his siblings. Though he chose not to pursue a higher education, he did use his portion of the fund to get vocational training and encouraged his younger siblings to take advantage of the savings their parents had accumulated for college or vocational training.

Overcoming Limiting Beliefs

It can take time to discover the beliefs you carry. Most of all, though, it takes willingness to do so. This is the first, and the most profound, step. When you are willing to acknowledge you have thoughts that do not serve your goals, you can observe and grow in your awareness of them. Ultimately, you can choose not to be driven by these thoughts and instead pursue a more effective path of thought.

Of all the choices you can make to overcome limiting self-talk, the most powerful is to choose what you prefer to tell yourself instead. What do you want to be saying to yourself about money? Remember when my coach challenged me about being "bad with money"? She asked me not to tell myself I was bad with money for one week. So I had to choose something else to tell myself. I decided on two phrases: "I'm willing to be good with money" and "I'm willing to learn what I need to know about money."

You see, if I had replaced, "I'm bad with money," with the opposite words, "I'm good with money," I wouldn't have believed myself. By saying, "I am willing to be good with money," I left myself room to begin a new and more empowering conversation with myself. At first, the old thoughts came out of habit. Over and over I had to catch myself in mid-thought and remind myself not to say I was bad with money. Gradually, I replaced the "bad with money" thought with "I am willing." It took time, but that effort proved to be worthwhile.

Consider taking on the challenge to listen and discover what those who are successful with their money tell themselves about their wealth. If you hear them say self-limiting words, don't take that on, but observe instead how those thoughts could be limiting. Keep talking to other people until you find the ones who have strong, positive beliefs about money, and take on those beliefs instead.

You may find you are surrounded almost entirely by people who have negative beliefs about money. That was certainly true when Brandy started looking for role models. Her immediate family could not provide the examples she needed, so she looked elsewhere for inspiration. If this is the case for you, you may have to watch documentaries or read books about successful people. Examine what they tell themselves. One treasure of a book to explore is *The Science of Getting Rich* by Wallace Wattles. It was published in 1910, so the writing style may seem dated, yet the concepts are just as powerful today and provide an excellent road map for changing both how you think, and how you can act on that thinking. I've found myself reading it over and over through the years, and I discover something new every time. My mentor suggests particularly reading chapters 4, 7, 11, and 14 in Wattles' book. We've made a practice of reading those chapters every day for ninety days, so that the knowledge seeps in at a profound level. This may be more of a challenge than you are willing to take on right now. Still, keep it in mind as a powerful practice.

In any event, seek out what you would choose to believe if you were to be fully conscious and effective with your money. This is a powerful step toward making peace with your money.

Changing your thinking is a crucial first step to moving from monetary insufficiency to monetary sufficiency. The next step is to examine how you behave with money and consciously choose actions and behaviors that support financial sufficiency.

Peace with Money Activities

Activity One

- The objective of this exercise is to encourage you to see any additional self-limiting conversations that are keeping you from experiencing peace with money.
- Complete the following steps:
- Review the money autobiography you wrote for chapter 3.
- Observe what you said about money in your autobiography. Highlight anything that seems to narrow or reduce your options.
- Next, review what you wrote about your current situation for chapter 4. Again, look for any thoughts that could be limiting you and write them down.

- Review the notes you've taken regarding your self-talk about money. Add anything you may have missed.

Activity Two

Look at each self-limiting thought you listed from your money autobiography (from chapter 3) and your current situation (from chapter 4) and address them one by one. Do the following:

- Consider alternatives to your self-talk. If you were to shift from what you currently say to yourself to something more in accord with how you want your self-talk to be, what would you say to yourself instead? For example, when I believed I was bad with money, I felt defeated and powerless. When I began to tell myself I wasn't bad with money, but that there were just things I didn't know yet, I began to be less attached to feeling powerless and more curious about learning what I needed to know. I became happier about learning new ways of dealing with money.

- Write out some new beliefs that you are willing to practice so you can replace the old ones. Consider putting these new thoughts where you can read them every day. Then make the commitment to do so. After all, it's your empowerment you're after! This will help activate your new thoughts. Then the new, empowering thoughts can replace the old, self-defeating thoughts.

Additional Resources

- *The Science of Getting Rich* by Wallace Wattles.
- Refer to the free *Make Peace with Money Workbook* at www.makepeacewithmoney.com, Lesson 5. Log in with the username *makepeacewithmoney* and the password *peace42*.

Chapter 6

MOVING FROM INSUFFICIENCY TO SUFFICIENCY

Honor your desire for a new life. Say yes to the small inklings of interest and curiosity that present themselves each day.

—Lynn A. Robinson

The fear of not having enough is an intriguing phenomenon prevalent in the United States. It is seen when a person has a job, a home, a refrigerator and cupboards filled with food, transportation, a closet full of clothing, and expendable cash, yet the individual complains about being "so broke." They may not be able to buy the new kayak they want and have debt to deal with, but this outright disregard for the wealth they actually have is a problem of perception more than reality. Our culture encourages the acquisition of more and more things, and we tend to compare ourselves to others (who may appear to be better off than we are). Americans often have the misconception that more is better, and many feel they don't have "enough."

What we perceive and believe about our circumstances effect how we behave. It is common to hear people say, "I can't afford it," or, "I just don't have the money." We often believe ourselves to be genuinely poor when clearly we are not. What's more likely is that we aren't managing the money we have with clarity. We are not guiding our own lives based on our values, intentions, and goals.

We may not be able to afford something at the moment. Yet if what we want is sufficiently important, with planning and effort, we can usually save or earn the extra money required. Reaching a spending goal takes clarity about what you desire and the will to stick with a plan of action toward obtaining it.

When we look at real poverty globally, the statistics can be sobering. According to the World Bank, nearly 800 million people, or approximately 10.5 percent of the world's population, live on less than $1.90 per day.[14] This figure alone should be enough to remind us of just how tilted our thinking gets when we worry about money.

But is information enough? We tend to compare ourselves to our peers or to images of our culture in contemporary advertising, film, and social media more than we identify with the truly poor of this world. The more we remain disconnected and fail to recognize the genuine poverty existing in the world, the more likely we are to keep ourselves in a consciousness that says we are lacking in money.

This whole conversation can be distilled to one choice: you can either focus your mind-set on scarcity, lack, and fear, or you can choose to concentrate your thoughts on well-being, sufficiency, faith, and love. You can choose to see yourself as financially impoverished—disregarding the plenitude of things you already have—or you can choose to see your life as bountiful and growing ever richer.

Let's look at the evidence. If you focus on lack, then "not enough" is what you'll see. Yet does that mean your life is lacking? Are

---

14   "Poverty Headcount Ratio at $1.90 a Day (2011 PPP) (Percent of Population," The World Bank, accessed July 30, 2018, https://data.worldbank. org/indicator/SI.POV.DDAY.

you aware of what happens before you even take a sip of your morning brew? It's likely that potable water streams out every time you open the faucet. Electricity powers your lights, cell phone, tablet, and coffee maker at the flip of a switch. What about the beauty of the sun streaming through the window or the song of the birds chirping outside? Or, conversely, the patter of much-needed rain? When you focus on lack, you may not even notice the value of the sun, the birds, or the rain at all.

Encourage yourself to examine the evidence you've gathered to support your conclusions. Seek to determine what is actually true. When you can see what is really there before you, rather than focusing on a conclusion you've leaped to, you can choose what you want to think. You'll begin to seek out sound evidence to support your preferred thoughts.

Insufficiency or Sufficiency?

A person experiencing a scarcity mind-set might begin her day like this: She arises feeling tired and mutters the familiar refrain, "I didn't get enough sleep." This is the first scarcity thought.

She goes to the kitchen to make coffee. She forgot to buy coffee beans and has to use instant coffee. Not at all the fragrant cup she anticipated. She reaches for the milk, only to discover her teenage son pouring the last of it over his cereal. Now her coffee is really not how she wants it. "There's never enough milk in the fridge," she grumbles to herself. Scarcity thought number two.

She looks at that day's to-do list. It's several items long and she thinks, "How can I ever fit all this in? I don't have time." Scarcity thought number three.

As her son goes out the door, he asks, "Can I have $20 for my aikido class? Today's the last day I can pay this month." When she forgot to get coffee she also forgot to cash a check. "It's my last $20," she thinks. And the scarcity game has a firm hold on yet another day.

Entrenched in a scarcity mind-set, she sits down to pay bills and sees there's not enough in her account to pay them. "Oh no," she thinks. "Short again this month." Deeper into scarcity emotions she goes, believing there is never enough and unable to see how there could possibly ever be.

Let's play out this same scenario with a person who is committed to living with a sufficiency mind-set: She awakens and spies the sun peeking in the window. She stretches and enjoys the loveliness for a moment. She also had a short night's sleep. "I'm tired," she thinks, "but I'm so grateful the sun is shining today."

In the kitchen, she realizes she neglected to buy her favorite coffee beans the day before. She says, "I'm glad I bought this instant coffee to make in a pinch." She also sees that her son has used the last of the milk. Though she's momentarily annoyed, she refocuses and tells him, "I'm happy to see you're eating break-fast—I know you usually skip." She puts an ice cube in her coffee and enjoys it black. She is more interested in peace and harmony for herself and her family than she is in being cranky or achieving immediate gratification.

With her abundance mind-set, she goes to her scheduler and sees the work she's outlined for the day. While there are many tasks, since she has a practice of living in abundance, she makes sure to address her highest priorities first to have a sense of ease about her day. She knows some of the lower-priority tasks may not get done until tomorrow or even next week, but she says quietly, "It's okay. Everything will get done."

The woman takes a couple of deep breaths to summon a feeling of expansiveness. When her son asks for $20, she says, "You enjoy aikido so much I'm glad I can support you in taking it." She leaves home a few minutes early so she can stop at the ATM, grateful she doesn't have to wait until the bank opens.

After a full day of noticing things she can be grateful for—from a parking spot next to the ATM to finding her favorite coffee on sale—she sits down to do her finances. She checks her bank account. Despite her overall abundance mind-set, she is still paying down debt she accrued several years earlier. She balances her checkbook and adds up her bills.

She realizes a payment for $396 is due and she doesn't have enough to pay it and wonders how she'll cover it. Then she realizes she billed a client several weeks earlier for $500 that, despite her careful record keeping, she had nearly forgotten about. She calls the client and requests he pay online. He is able to pay only $250 and promises to pay the remainder the following week. With what remains in her account plus her client's payment, she is happy to now have enough to pay the $396. Even if she had not received the $250, she knows she is more likely to find a solution to a shortfall when choosing to think from a positive rather than struggling mind-set.

Can you feel the difference between these mind-sets?

Changing perception alone does not summon the physical reality of money. However, when you are in a scarcity mind-set, you are much less open to innovative solutions, learning from others, or even responding well to opportunities that may be right before you. You are less likely to seek out healthy action steps to address the problem and more likely to just complain. Beyond being closed to receiving, when you struggle, you are also less likely to have the clarity needed to plan, envision, and take actions that support you in reaching your goals and, ultimately, realizing financial well-being.

When you approach your life with a deep understanding that all is well, you'll see a world filled with plenty, even though you may experience a shortage in the moment. You'll have less doubt and fear about your ability to create well-being for yourself, whether in relation to money or other areas of your life. When you focus on an abundance or sufficiency mind-set, you realize there are enough resources to support us all and, most importantly, you are grateful for that which you have.

Sure, you may still have debt you are paying down. You may not be driving a Tesla, or even a car manufactured in this decade, but let me ask you: Does your pantry have food? Do you have a roof over your head? Do you have an iPad, smartphone, and other basic toys indicative of a comfortable lifestyle? Do you have running water and electricity in uninterrupted supply? Do you have an education? Do you have skills and resources you can apply to earn money? Do you have friends, colleagues, or loved ones who are supportive?

You may have only a few of these. However, you may have other things you can count as your own personal form of wealth. Frankly, even just a few belongings, along with an abundance mind-set, can add up to a rewarding life filled with richness.

We too easily overlook the abundance right before our eyes because scarcity (the sense that there is "never enough") has become an overarching paradigm of thought in Western culture. Comparing ourselves to others and their belongings feeds this "never enough" thought pattern. Judging our plenty, or lack of it, based solely on monetary wealth or number of possessions limits our capacity to free ourselves from scarcity.

In the excellent book *Abundance*, authors Peter Diamandis and Steven Kotler reveal, through extensive research, that there is enough of everything—natural resources, money, water, land, technology—for every single individual on the planet to be fed, to be housed, to have access to clean water, and to have an income.[15] It is the scarcity mind-set with which we think about the resources and then how we utilize those resources that is the problem. The authors invite us to rethink how we humans use and distribute the resources we have.

Using resources responsibly and giving out of our abundance begins modestly, at home and within ourselves. Our ability to see ourselves as beings of true abundance, not lacking for anything, is fundamental to our ability to use and distribute our own resources in the most effective possible way. We'll be better stewards of our money and possessions overall when we change our thinking and then behave accordingly.

As you come to recognize when your own thought patterns turn to doubt, fear, or scarcity, it can be helpful to define what wealth is to you. I encourage you to widen your scope to examine that which you might not ordinarily explore.

Redefine Wealth

To some, wealth may include a yacht, a mansion, and fancy dinners. However, what about the wealth of healthy cells in your body? The knowledge and potential of a healthy mind? What about the wealth visible in nature—in trees fruiting each summer,

---

15   Peter H. Diamandis and Steven Kotler, *Abundance: The Future Is Better Than You Think*, 2nd ed. (New York: Free Press, 2014).

fields growing food that feed us, the glorious wilderness areas and parks abundant throughout the world where we can nourish our minds and spirits?

Would you not agree you are wealthy if you have a loving partner and a network of family and friends with whom you enjoy supportive relationships? Are you wealthy if you have time to take the kids to soccer practice or play Frisbee golf with friends on a Saturday afternoon? So much evidence of prosperity and abundance exists around us if we are willing to let ourselves see it.

A Coaching Story: Matthew Experiences Abundance

When we last discussed Matthew, he was in debt to the tune of $72,000 and just beginning to work with me as his financial coach. That summer, he reconnected with some of his associates from his days as a runaway and they decided to go to a Rainbow Gathering.

When Matthew was in his teens, he went to a Rainbow Gathering with some other street people. They hitched a ride and Matthew found himself out in the woods eating a concoction of beans and rice with other travelers. At the time, he took a good deal for granted. He was fed, given clean water, and even offered a sleeping bag. And, while it seemed like quite an adventure, he also found himself feeling cranky, unsafe, and unwilling to graciously receive what was offered. As a teenager striking out on his own, he wanted to demonstrate he could take care of himself. He was afraid of others' generosity and wondered what they might really want from him. That was then.

This time, Matthew went to the Rainbow Gathering as a grown man and college grad. He packed a duffle bag with essentials and extra food to share. Even though he'd been to a Rainbow Gathering before, he was astonished to see the abundance present at the gathering. He was given free food everywhere he went, and he freely shared what he'd brought as well. He went to Hobo Alley, a Rainbow kitchen where many young runaways congregated. He was served coffee by a young boy not much older than he had been when he was last at a Gathering. He was greeted by an abundance of warmth and community.

Matthew realized how, as an angry teenager, he'd been driven by a scarcity mind-set. This summer, experiencing the camp as a man, he saw abundance in a whole new way. When we resumed our coaching, he shared that the scarcity thoughts that had gripped him for so long had loosened. Even though few people at the gathering had much money, Matthew came to see the difference between poverty consciousness and an abundant and sharing mind-set. He began to turn his attention to resolving his money issues.

As you take steps to gain greater effectiveness in your handling of money and seek to change your mind-set, a natural result is that you'll see your life from a more abundant viewpoint. You'll redefine what true wealth is for you, celebrate what you already have, and lay a foundation for more peace and wealth in your life. The exercises at the end of this chapter and in the *Make Peace with Money Workbook*, Lesson 6, will help you accomplish this.

Changing your thoughts and beliefs is one thing, but making the deeper shift needed so that the change truly lasts can be challenging. That said, consistency and devotion to this task is among the most rewarding work you can do. Let's look at some ways to shift the way you think. You may decide to take yourself by the hand and agree to change. You could choose to be willing to be vigilant in discovering what you think and say and then change those conversations that no longer serve you. Meditation and affirmation practices can be highly effective toward such a change.

You may choose to work one-to-one with a financial coach, or you may pursue a spiritual practice. In addition, you can study inspiring leaders in business, learn mindfulness principles, or cultivate a deep sense of curiosity about how positive technologies and people are changing the world. Any of these options can serve to open your thinking and expand your awareness.

Shifting from a scarcity to a sufficiency mind-set means observing and adapting your attitude along with injecting a large dose of gratitude. Neither works well without the other. Should you actually not have enough money, then there are some other factors that come into play. The pathway to change is this:

- Gain clarity about your situation by looking to see exactly what you owe, what you own, your income, and the other resources you have.

- Develop your financial vision by stating clearly what it is you want to be different in regard to your money and overall wealth.

- Take small actions consistently that move you toward your financial vision.

- Practice an affirming attitude toward yourself and money; activate a belief that you can be, do, and have what you want.

- Express gratitude for and celebrate what you already have and that which you receive. When practiced consistently, gratitude becomes a path to living more gracefully.

For now, though, let's start with exercises that are aimed at helping you step out of insufficiency and into a way of life that is sufficient, even abundant.

Peace with Money Activities

Activity One

- For one week, each day list three things you are grateful for.

- At the end of the week, read the gratitude notes you've made. Notice especially those that contribute to a sense of well-being. Do the things you are grateful for reflect richness in your life? Are the things you are grateful for occurring in the moment? Or do they recur regularly?

- Pick one or two things you are grateful for and celebrate that they are in your life. You might celebrate by speaking with another about it. Or purchase a lovely flower and plant it in your garden, or take a walk in the park or at a beach. Choose some celebrations that cost little or no money. What would be a delightful celebration of what is going well in your life?

Activity Two

- What empowering ways of being do you choose to take on? (Empowering choices about money include learning what you need to know to resolve your money challenges and devotion to action that will better your situation.)

- Start taking small actions consistently to move toward where you want to be with money. Begin with an affirmative attitude toward yourself and money, and express gratitude. This begins as a practice but may become a way of life as you experience the benefits.

Additional Resources

- Refer to the free *Make Peace with Money Workbook* at www.makepeacewithmoney.com, Lesson 6. Log in with the username *makepeacewithmoney* and the password *peace42*.

- *Abundance: The Future Is Better Than You Think* and *Bold: How to Go Big, Create Wealth, and Impact the World* by Peter H. Diamandis and Steven Kotler.

- *Building Your Field of Dreams* by Mary Manin Morrissey.

- *Ask and It Is Given: The Teachings of Abraham* by Esther Hicks.

Chapter 7
A POSITIVE RELATIONSHIP WITH MONEY

*To forgive is to set a prisoner free and discover
that the prisoner was you.*

—Lewis B. Smedes

Once you actively take steps to integrate an abundance mind-set into your everyday life, the next step is to start building your attitudinal muscles with forgiveness and gratitude.

When we hold on to grudges, hurts, and anger, we limit our own range of possibility. When I first was learning about making peace with money, I had been holding on to some deep hurt and hostility against a man who had abused me in my childhood. Every time I thought about the man, I cringed and felt both rage and pain. Because he was someone who was fairly close to our family, whenever I was around anyone who was related to him, I felt angry and diminished.

When my financial coach suggested that I might want to forgive my abuser, I flew into yet another rage. "Forgive! Do you *know* what he did to me?" I yelled. She persisted in her suggestion, and I am so glad she did. Once I had done the forgiveness work, I could see that I was the one who had been a prisoner to my hurt and rage. By the time I forgave him, the man had been dead for several years. Yet I'd been packing around my ill will all that time. My lack of forgiveness limited my peace with others and myself, and it affected so many of my decisions.

Throughout my life, I'd told myself, "I'm damaged goods, so I'll never be a success. No one would want someone like me on their team or in their life." With this skewed thinking, I spent money on items I didn't need, just to comfort myself. I also limited my ability to earn, often feeling I wasn't worthy of asking for a raise at work.

After doing the forgiveness work, and once I really absorbed that I did not need to think and behave like that anymore, I was also able to be around my abuser's family and enjoy them for who they are: kind, generous people who would have been horrified if they'd known what he had done. And I was able to step into the freedom of not having to carry the rage for the rest of my life. I was free to discover what I wanted in the present and for my future, rather than dragging the past along with me. Shortly thereafter, with my newfound lightness, doors opened that have led me to this work I love so much.

Appreciating what we have and what we receive helps anchor a shift in attitude. And so does forgiveness. In fact, gratitude is the means by which you can complete the release you begin when you forgive. And gratitude can lead you closer to the source of good. Whether, like many, you acknowledge God as your source, or you simply realize that gratitude expressed to others around you makes your life and theirs better, gratitude generates well-being for you and others.

I'm so grateful my coach persisted in guiding me to forgiveness, for it freed me to examine my own well-being and discover how I could focus my newfound energy into improving my financial health. There is an excellent process for forgiveness in Maria

Nemeth's book, *The Energy of Money*.[16] Or a coach, counselor, or minister can guide you through the process.

I heartily encourage you to do as I did at that juncture and build the skills for managing money, such as getting a current snapshot of your financial situation, living within your budget, and managing your cash flow. Exercises to help you do these activities are found in the *Make Peace with Money Workbook*, Lesson 11. However, you may find little satisfaction in being proficient with your money until you actually feel at peace with it. This is a paradox because the better you manage your money, the more certainty you will gain about it. At the same time, the more you seek to be at peace with money, the more you will want to manage money well so you can experience even more peace with it. You'll see what your efforts are doing for you. This is why your thoughts about money and a grateful attitude are both fundamental and co-supportive to your well-being with money.

Monetarily Rich, yet so Poor

One of the saddest situations I've seen with money was Roxie, a woman who attended church dressed in faded clothing that had been stylish several decades earlier. She consistently put money in the offering plate, yet never more than $5. Rail thin, she ate sparingly, even at church potlucks, where there was plenty of food. She lived in a formerly elegant but now quite run-down three-story Victorian home she'd inherited from her father, who had inherited it from his father. Her grandfather had been successful in business and built the home to showcase his accomplishments. Her father had continued to thrive in the business and left the home to her. Those who knew Roxie feared she would lose it to

16   Maria Nemeth, *The Energy of Money: A Spiritual Guide to Financial and Personal Fulfillment* (New York: Ballantine, 1997), 200.

taxes one day. She always complained of how she wasn't sure her resources could support her for the rest of her life—I don't recall ever hearing her express gratitude for anything.

Roxie had no children, yet she had written a will, signed and witnessed by people who died before her, in which she left the bulk of her estate to a distant cousin. By his own account after her passing, they had never met or even spoken with each other. We were shocked to discover from her cousin that she'd received a substantial monthly income from investments her father had made many years earlier in highly successful companies.

Roxie had more than $3 million in investments and nearly another $1 million in her bank account, one which did not pay interest and which was insured only up to the federal limit. When her cousin prepared the house for sale, he discovered she had more than $100,000 in cash stashed in various cubbyholes, cookie jars, and jewelry and cigar boxes throughout the house. In addition, she had jewelry and antiques worth nearly $300,000.

Even as run-down as the house was, it was structurally sound, completely debt-free, and worth nearly $700,000. I could certainly understand Roxie's desire to keep the jewelry and antiques, for surely they had sentimental value to her. However, I was dismayed that she'd lived such an impoverished life even while having plenty of money that could have made her final years very comfortable. She was unable to appreciate the ease the money could bring her or to be grateful for the investments her father and grandfather had made on her behalf. And so she suffered. Was she wealthy? In money, yes. In everything else, not so much.

Even a millionaire, who may know the ins and outs of managing money yet experiences no peace with it, will struggle. Some, like Roxie, have inherited money but have never been taught how to manage it. Often they are afraid that others will take advantage of them and are fearful to ask for the support they need to learn how to manage it. They may be scared to give freely because they truly do not know how much "enough" actually is.

The experience of peace with money is more valuable than a six- or seven-figure income. Don't get me wrong—a substantial income is worth developing and maintaining, particularly if you want a lifestyle that supports significant belongings, extensive traveling, or generous giving. Yet when you express gratitude for all that is well in your life and for the precious gift of being at peace with money, you'll feel much richer—regardless of your level of income.

The Value of Gratitude

The more you consciously cultivate a feeling of gratitude for all you have, the more at peace you will feel. As I've practiced gratitude, I've come to see that I'm even grateful for things I once thought were terrible difficulties.

While I am not particularly grateful to have lost money during the dot-com bubble, I am extremely grateful to have had the *experience* of losing substantial amounts of money. Of course, I'd love to have that money now! But I realize that experience set me on the path to become a financial coach and has given me a great deal of compassion for my clients, many of whom have made significant mistakes with money or have lost a lot of it.

I'm also grateful for experiences I've had with my life partners. Some of those experiences were marvelous. Some of them were excruciating. Yet the sum total of those experiences has given me a broader view of what I don't want, as well as what I find good and wholesome. Would I prefer not to have experienced pain in those relationships? Of course! But I welcome the learning that came out of the pain. It gives me spaciousness to understand the challenges that others, including my clients, are having and to help them deal with those challenges.

I've chosen to learn from my mistakes and I encourage you to do so as well. Some people believe that a person who's had a generally negative attitude his or her entire adult life cannot change to see things in a more positive light. Yet I know two people, Johann, a man in his mid-fifties, and Serena, a woman in her late forties, unacquainted with each other and from different countries. Before we met, each had experienced a great deal of pain stemming from their life circumstances, including their rela-tionship with money. Both made a conscious choice to change their attitude from negative to positive. They chose to address their money challenges with clarity and in a straightforward manner, following the guidance from chapter 11 and the cor-responding Lesson 11 in the workbook. Even more valuable, though, were their choices to keep a gratitude journal in which they wrote three things they were grateful for each day.

About six months after Johann started keeping his gratitude journal, he wrote this note to me:

I never realized until now the power of gratitude. It lifts me up when I'm down. I'm even learning to be grateful for things I find difficult. I'd been putting off balancing my accounts and asking for a raise for years. Taking care of those things was hard. I thought I couldn't do it, but then I did; it was so rewarding. I got a raise, even more than I asked for. And it's so good to know where I stand with my accounts. Thank you for starting me on this path. Even though I still get down on myself sometimes, I'm feeling more positive than I ever have in my whole life!

Serena's story was a little different. She'd experienced severe health issues beginning in early adulthood that created quite a vacuum in her finances. She was only able to pay for bare necessities after medical expenses. This is how she'd lived for twenty-six years until we began working together (her coaching was a gift from a friend who knew Serena was getting well and wanted to support a better life for her). Understandably, Serena was depressed and despairing of ever having a life that was different from the one she'd experienced to date, especially as it concerned money. Her day-to-day mood was gloomy. Though things seemed tough, I suggested that she begin a gratitude journal, looking for even the tiniest things that gave her pleasure or supported her well-being.

Like Johann, Serena emailed me a few months later...

The first thing I wrote in my gratitude journal was about my friend and her gift. The next was for rainbows in soap bubbles in the kitchen sink when I was doing my dishes. Some days I didn't know what to write and I'd sit and stare at the page for long minutes. But then something silly would come up. I'd write it with a chuckle. After a while, I found myself being grateful during the day when I wasn't at my journal. And then I began to tell others what I appreciated— things like, 'Thanks for checking me out so quickly' to the clerk at the grocery. And I began to feel even better. Not only am I getting well physically, but I'm healing my attitude as well. What a blessing!

In fact, at least thirty studies have shown that older people who rate higher on positive-attitude measures tend to live longer than those who have fewer positive thoughts, says Sarah Pressman, assistant professor of psychology and social behavior at the University of California, Irvine. Pressman searched autobiographies of eighty-eight noted psychologists. She found those who described their lives with more positive emotions lived up to six years longer on average than the psychologists who tended to be melancholy.[17] Positive psychology is a quickly growing field of study and counseling. A key component to developing a more positive attitude is expressing your gratitude.

While the choice to systematically become more positive is a decision that takes dedication, focus, and practice, gratitude is an effective way to open the door to becoming gentler with yourself. Gratitude is a pleasant feeling, one that can contribute to a sense of peace. And the more you focus on gratitude and peace in a day, the better your day can go.

You may say, as Debbie, the daughter of a friend, recently did, "But Lorna. There is nothing—*nothing*—in my life to be grateful for. I don't have any money and when I do my partner spends it. I live in a dump and my partner's unemployed and a whiner. I've got $43,000 in college loans to pay off, my car just broke down, and I work at a fast-food joint for minimum wage. And I have a second job cleaning houses on my days off. What do you suggest I do?"

The life this young woman outlined to me seemed pretty grim. First, I noticed that she was not homeless, though her circumstances seemed quite minimal. She had a job. She had college loans to pay, yes, but she also had a college education. It wasn't that her life was completely lacking. What was more accurate is that it lacked what she wanted for herself.

Over several conversations with Debbie, I suggested that she consider being grateful that she knows she wants to change her circumstances. Or she might appreciate the roof over her head.

---

17   Sarah D. Pressman and S. Cohen, "Positive Emotion Word Use and Longevity in Famous Deceased Psychologists," *Health Psychology* 31, no. 3 (2011): 297–305, http://dx.doi.org/10.1037/a0025339.

Viewed from a different perspective, we learn that, while her partner is unemployed and sometimes he complains about their lives, he also keeps the apartment clean and tidy, shops carefully and economically, and cooks so there are meals for her when she gets home from work.

Once Debbie started looking at her life differently, she realized how much she enjoys the ride she gets from her neighbor, whose job is near her workplace. She loves how nice it is to have good food prepared for her. And she's beginning to look for work with a nonprofit organization to put her education to work. She's found that when she works for a nonprofit for a certain number of years, a significant portion of her college loans will be forgiven. Debbie realizes she has always loved to be of service. Now that service will serve a double purpose.

Another example of the power of gratitude is a program carried out in the slums of Nairobi, Kenya, called the Africa Yoga Project. Most of the youth and young adults in the program, ages 18–35, come from impoverished backgrounds; many have lived on the streets since adolescence. They undergo an extensive certification program to become yoga teachers as a means to improve their lives and build a viable career.

The mentor-teachers know that before people can change their lives, they must stop blaming others for their circumstances. Once the students see it doesn't benefit them or others to place blame, they make choices to change their lives for the better. Once certified in yoga, these young adults teach classes for income. A condition of the program, which is free to those with little or no income, is that they teach at least one class to other impoverished youth so they can pass on what they've learned. Most are grateful to have this opportunity and welcome the chance to help others change their lives.

Wallace Wattles, author of *The Science of Getting Rich*, said, "It is necessary, then, to cultivate the habit of being grateful for every good thing that comes to you; and to give thanks continuously. And because all things have contributed to your advancement, you should include all things in your gratitude."[18]

So take the time to be grateful. Gratitude is a peaceful emotion, and people who are already living at peace with their money know the power of gratitude for whatever amount of money they have.

When looking for something to be grateful for, start small. It could be the voice of a songbird. A delicious meal. A podcast you listen to about something that interests you. The fresh new toothbrush the dentist just gave you. What is one thing you are grateful for right now?

The more grateful you are for what you have, and the more you act with gratitude, the more blessings show up to arouse your gratitude. Some people question the validity of this statement; however, I encourage you to try it out. A person who chooses to delight in small things will find themselves encountering an endless parade of small things to delight in. And that gives positive energy to their days. Usually, after a few weeks of delighting in small things, you'll discover there are few truly small things. On the other hand, a person who laments all of the things that go wrong in their day will only continue to bring forth more things to lament.

If you find yourself having a difficult time thinking of things to be grateful for, I encourage you to begin a practice of daily inspirational readings. Two books with I've found especially inspiring

18 Wallace Wattles, *The Science of Getting Rich* (n.p.: First Start Publishing e-edition, 2012), 36.

are Sarah Ban Breathnach's book *Simple Abundance* and Mary Mackenzie's book, *Peaceful Living: Daily Meditations for Living with Love, Healing, and Compassion.* (Mackenzie's book comes from her extensive study and teaching of compassionate communication and has been influential in gaining greater peace in my life and with money.)

The Power of Giving

When you feel grateful for what you have, you usually become more willing to give. When you realize that money is simply energy and, whether money is given or received, is nothing more than a form of energetic exchange, you'll understand that hoarding your money out of a scarcity mind-set actually inhibits the flow of its energy to you. There is great power in the act of giving. Even a smile, given fully and willingly, can change a person's day.

Being truly grateful for what you have increases your feelings of being at peace with money, pushes back against poverty consciousness, and stimulates you to give more of yourself, your money, your time, your resources. Giving, with no attachment to what you might receive: now there's a worthy aim. Indeed, one of the major advantages to cultivating peace with money is the ability to give fearlessly, not worrying about whether you have enough, because you'll have knowledge about and comfort with your finances.

We tend to feel good when we contribute to someone or something that we value. You can start by giving any amount that works for you. For some, it's giving one-tenth of their income. For others, it is a specific amount of time or money, given each week or month. The key, though, is to give consistently. Giving, supported by trust in the abundance that fills our lives and gratitude for our plenty, engages the flow of money.

Let me show you how this might work. Lucy had three small children, was unemployed, and lived on public assistance. She came to a free class I taught about peace with money at a local women's club. Inspired, she decided to give a dollar each week to the local food kitchen. Soon the leaders at the kitchen became aware of this consistent donation. They sought her out because that kind of consistency is what they needed from employees in the kitchen. She soon found herself no longer relying on public support and on a career track as a cook, something she'd always loved to do but had never thought of as a career. Lucy hadn't thought of receiving any good from her donation other than the satisfaction of feeling that she had enough to be able to give.

Keep in mind it is best not to cultivate the thought of giving in order to receive; indeed, that attitude changes the very act of giving. What we receive from any act of giving may not come back in that moment or from that same person. And we may never be able to trace a result from any single act of giving.

In fact, Lucy's case is an exception. It's much more usual that we'll notice a response that comes from somewhere other than where we gave. Whether what we receive is monetary or another form of goodness, it can come from all kinds of places and when we least expect it. It comes from our openness to receiving. Are you willing, right now, to begin discovering your giving "muscle"? Are you willing to exercise it without any thought as to what you may receive in return? Don't feel badly if your answer is no. Sometimes we must say no to something before we can authentically answer yes.

The power of giving is not to be underestimated. In a world

where people so often focus on what they want or need, you may occasionally find yourself longing to give. In fact, if you wanted to give something to another person and they were not open to receive it, you might feel frustrated. Giving and receiving are equally important actions, part of the interactive flow of energy and money.

When you are at peace with money, you are likely to feel more at ease and be more willing to give, again because you have clarity about your monetary situation. When you aren't at peace with your money, a request for a donation can feel annoying. Being at peace with money means being free to look at whether giving is right for you at that moment. Should you choose not to give money, you can still wish the person or the venture well, giving of the energy of your good thoughts instead of your monetary wealth. Or you may choose to give of your knowledge through mentoring or your time through service.

To keep the energetic flow going with money, it is important to consider giving outside of the context of it. Too often, when we are parsimonious with our money, we also hoard our energy; for example, if we feel our time is limited, we will be less likely to offer to help a friend or volunteer in our community. Money and time are two sides of the same coin, and experiencing scarcity in one usually contributes to a sense of scarcity in the other. However, giving time, even if only for a moment, can be enough to make a significant difference to another person.

Some time ago, I was going through a particularly stressful period. I'd been laid off from my job during a time of high unemployment and felt depressed. My demeanor was dour. My coach challenged me to give something away each day. I balked, saying, "Don't you know? I've just been laid off. I'm broke!" She smiled broadly as she replied, "Of course I know that." Then she asked me to find at least one smile to give away each day for thirty days. To say it was difficult at first would be an understatement. I didn't think I could do it and the first few smiles were pretty tentative. Yet I stayed committed to smiling at someone at least once each day.

To my surprise, I was soon looking for opportunities to smile at people, discovering the delight I felt when they returned the smile. About three weeks into the challenge, a harried-looking older woman stopped me and said, "Do you know how long it has been since anyone really looked at me and smiled? I can't recall the last time. You've made my day, dear. Keep smiling." I'll never forget that. What is the cost of a smile, after all? A mere moment to boost a person's mood for the day? The cost is minimal but the returns are high.

Recognize the power of giving in your own life, and the joy you take in giving to others. Contrast this feeling with the fear and need to grasp or hold on in perceived "tight" times. Which is more expansive? Which brings more peace? Generating gratitude and letting it guide you to giving is a powerful tool available to all of us for use in seeking peace with money.

Peace with Money Activities

- If you haven't already started a gratitude notebook, do so now. Each morning, write three things you are grateful for in your life. This sets a tone of appreciation at the beginning of the day.

- In your notebook, write three things you are grateful for at the end of each day. It can be the same items you listed in the morning or things that occurred during your day.

- Consider sharing your practice with others through having a moment of gratitude before each meal you eat together, with each sharing one thing each of you is grateful for.

- Whenever you start to experience scarcity or any other charged emotion around money, pause, breathe, close your eyes, and summon a feeling of gratitude by thinking about one specific thing you are thankful for. It could be as simple as air to breathe. Using gratitude to ease out of fearful or negative emotions around money can be an effective tool.

Additional Resources

- Refer to the free *Make Peace with Money Workbook* at www.makepeacewithmoney.com, Lesson 7. Log in with the username *makepeacewithmoney* and the password *peace42*.

- *Simple Abundance: A Daybook of Comfort and Joy* by Sarah Ban Breathnach.

- *Peaceful Living: Daily Meditations for Living with Love, Healing, and Compassion* by Mary Mackenzie.

- Africa Yoga Project (https://www.africayogaproject.org/pages/our-history).

Chapter 8

DISCOVERING THE PURPOSE YOU WANT YOUR MONEY TO SERVE

There is no favorable wind to the sailor who does not know where he wants to go.

—Seneca the Younger

If you've never written out a vision statement for your life, this chapter guides you in doing so. If you already have a vision statement, consider this as an opportunity to bring your vision up-to-date. We'll explore the cost of not having a vision and the purpose a vision can serve. You'll get instructions for writing yours, both for your life as a whole and for how money figures into your life.

Vision

Your vision is your game plan for life. Just as businesses commonly have their vision statements posted for employees and clients to see, you can create a similar vision for your life. You can keep it private if you wish, or you can share it with others you trust to support you in achieving it. Usually, it doesn't occur to us to create such a thing for ourselves, unless the idea is introduced by a counselor, coach, or friend. Yet when you create a vision statement and refer to it regularly, you will likely find your life starting to open up in purposeful directions.

Why is a vision important when the topic of this book is making peace with money? Without it, you may never truly achieve the peace you want in your life as a whole. You may believe you are a victim of circumstances and that you cannot be headed in the direction you most want to go. You may feel life hands you decisions rather than you making them.

The clearer you are about how you want your life to be, the more it is realistic to think you can bring what you most desire into actuality. The very exercise of creating your life and money vision is an act of courage and self-appreciation. When you clearly define what you want, you'll begin to see how you can achieve it. You'll take actions to clear any obstacles that come up. You may even seek the support of others to help you address them. And you'll take steps that will move you toward the life you want. You are a co-creator of your life; you need not be a reactor or victim. Having a vision and reading it regularly reminds you of this.

Simply put, your vision is your dream for yourself, written down on paper or noted digitally. It specifies what you want to bring into your world. It includes your highest aims and desires. When you write it, include the way you want to feel.

Do you remember daydreaming when you were in school? Did you kick that habit to the curb when you became an adult, thinking it was useless? It's not. In fact, engaging in a good day-dreaming session regularly can be profitable to your well-being. It's difficult, in the day-to-day rush of activity, to step back and look at our lives from a different angle. Imagining and daydreaming allows us to do just that, from a more relaxed perspective. It's crucial, though, that daydreaming is done with gentle direction so it doesn't spiral into ineffectual fantasy. Your imaginings form the foundation for your vision. In the *Make Peace with Money Workbook* Lesson 9, you'll find a guide to creating your vision.

The Cost of Not Having a Vision

Human beings crave a certain amount of clarity and direction in their lives. It is no accident that ancient and not-so-ancient tribes sent their youth on vision quests and why many adults go on such quests today as well.

Without a view of how you want your life to be, you may feel like you are at sea, undirected. If you don't have clear direction, it's difficult to make rewarding progress. Too many people stagnate because they don't see their next step. This is when many people disappear into binge-watching TV, endless gaming, living life through others, and even drinking or using drugs. Not to say there's anything wrong with watching shows, playing games, or having a drink now and then; the danger is when the behavior takes over and consumes your life.

Without some clarity about where you are headed, you are more likely to be reactive to life events rather than proactive. The cost is a life that is much like a sailboat set adrift with no sail and no one to steer. Your boat may or may not end up someplace useful, depending on the currents. Do you want to sail in a direction that serves you well? Or do you want to make do with whatever life presents? If you want to produce a reality you prefer, then writing out a vision for your life is invaluable.

What Purpose Might Your Vision Serve?

If you are striving for a life filled with greater peace, the vision you write can give you signposts and a road map to escort you on your way. It can act as a touchstone for who you truly are, your most authentic self, when you may have lost sight of yourself. For it to be a clear road map, however, it is vital that you know some things about yourself so you can include them in your vision.

To begin with, what are your most significant values? What speaks to the core of your integrity? Core values that speak to my integrity include love, compassion, kindness, empowering and supporting others, peace, courage, and creativity. What are yours? Think about times when you've been at your best. Who were you being in that moment? Were you gentle? Truthful? Joyous? Some other qualities?

How Your Values and Purpose Inform Your Goals

When you develop a goal that reflects your vision as well as your values and purpose, you'll experience coherence even as you begin to take the actions required to fulfill the goal. Your goals will seem more fulfilling because you are living within your integrity. If you haven't already done so, go to the *Make Peace with Money Workbook* and use the exercise found in Lesson 2 to define your values and purpose.

Some people seek to directly meet their desire for monetary riches or fame, without taking the time and energy to determine whether those desires are in context with the whole of what they want in life, which may be happiness and self-sufficiency. It may come as a surprise, but a drive for financial success is often a formula for anxiety and depression rather than happiness, a University of Rochester study suggests.[19] Recent graduates' achievements and levels of happiness were evaluated over a two

19   Christopher P. Niemiec, Richard M. Ryan, and Edward L. Deci, "The Path Taken: Consequences of Attaining Intrinsic and Extrinsic Aspirations in Post-College Life," *Journal of Research in Personality* 43, no. 3 (June 2009): 291–306, https://doi.org/10.1016/j.jrp.2008.09.001.

year period. Participant's goals were divided into two categories: (1) extrinsic (wealth, fame, and personal image) and (2) intrinsic (meaningful relationships, health, and personal growth).

Achieving intrinsic goals led to higher self-esteem and a greater sense of well-being, the analysis revealed. Contrary to the traditional American dream, attaining extrinsic goals of wealth and fame more often led to anxiety and unhappiness. The more people achieve their extrinsic goals, the more "they tend to feel like pawns, like they're on a treadmill running and not completely in charge of themselves," said Edward Deci, a coauthor of the study.[20]

As you create a vision that reflects your integrity and then generate goals based on that vision, you'll find that your vision and goals will help you be more consistently aware of what motivates you. Is what you actually want extrinsic, such as large sums of money, a fancy home, and an expensive automobile? Or are you guided by intrinsic motivations, such as a desire to learn something new, to enjoy physical well-being, or to be a loving person? Or do you possess some mix of outer and inner goals? In other words, who do you choose to be?

While there is nothing wrong with having high aspirations, it's crucial to a sense of well-being that they be the result of a principled life rather than solely the result of an acquisitive drive that produces angst.

You might choose an intention such as being a loving parent or to regularly express your joy. These could be intentions vital to your well-being. You may intend to be a good provider, financially

---

20 "Key to Happiness? It's Not Money or Looks," LiveScience, NBCNews. com, last updated June 2, 2009, http://www.nbcnews.com/id/31067143/ns/ health-behavior/t/key-happiness-its-not-money-or-looks/#.W4iAZehKhPY.

independent, or at ease with money. Or you may intend on being a mentor, teacher, or activist. Many of us possess intentions that contribute to our sense of well-being. Your intentions point to purpose, which gives meaning to life.

For example, my neighbor loves to create beauty and has a lovely flower garden that everyone in the neighborhood enjoys. A friend loves being a grandmother so much that her license plate holder says, "Grandma on board." A colleague who has a lot of experience as a coach recently became a mentor for other coaches. And a young man I know has an intention to be a healing massage therapist.

What are your highest priorities? What greater purpose will your intentions serve? How might you want to incorporate what you intend for your life into your vision?

If your life vision depicts you living the most authentic life you can imagine, and if you consistently focus on that vision, you are more likely to realize that version of yourself.

While you may want to change the world, the reality is that we must bring out the best in ourselves first. A peace-filled life can have a profound impact on those with whom you come into contact each day. This is one of many marvelous purposes your vision can serve!

If you are unclear right now about your purpose and vision and how they will serve you, know you are not alone. It often takes people a few tries before they get a vision statement that fully reflects what they actually desire.

Writing Your Vision to Affect the Present

When you write your vision, write it in the present tense, as if it is already real. Then read it every day for thirty days. Look for what already actually exists and acknowledge—even celebrate—that you have already achieved it. Decide on one or more small steps you can take right away to bring the portions of your vision that have not yet occurred into reality. Tiny actions, taken each day (or even on most days), add up to significant change over time. Start now!

Writing my vision has been a required assignment for a number of coaching courses I've taken through the years. At first, I thought of it as a dream that would magically occur sometime in the future if I would just keep on keeping on. What I wrote sometimes felt unattainable, like it was out there waiting to happen, but somehow, never quite present. Understandably, much of it stayed in the future, not yet achieved.

My current vision describes both what is already present and right in my life as well as desires I still wish to fulfill, the ways of being I have yet to achieve. When I read this vision, which I do for thirty days in a row two or three times a year, I read it as if it is already real. I lean into it to sense how my achieved vision feels. For the five months I was writing the first draft of this book, I chose to read my vision every day to inspire myself because this project was an unrealized goal for a long time. During the time it took to write this book, I was being proactive to bring the part of my vision that says "I am a published author" into reality.

I take some action on as much of my vision as I possibly can every day, even if it is only a tiny, tiny step. Recently, when I had several meetings and coaching appointments, I was able to spend only about five minutes on the book project. I spent that few minutes revising a couple of sentences. Though a tiny step, it was satisfying in that those sentences are now clearer and I fulfilled my commitment to work on the book consistently.

Once you've written your vision statement, I recommend that you do the same. If you read your vision statement and then take action toward it each day, you'll likely discover new possibilities opening up that can help you achieve that vision. When your attention is on both what you want and on what is working for you already, your goals are fresh in your mind. You will be more likely to discover opportunities to move toward those goals.

Say, for example, that you've always wanted to take an Alaskan Inside Passage cruise. You may hear someone at a party talking about a special Alaska tour that is 20 percent off the regular price. By talking with them you discover it's scheduled the exact dates you want to go. Or you may have envisioned a particular way you want your home to look and then you hear about someone who has been transferred and needs to get rid of their nearly new belongings quickly (and at far less than they would cost new). You discover that their furnishings fit neatly into your vision.

Perhaps one of the most valuable things you'll discover through having a clear vision is that you can focus on the way you want to *be* in your life rather than the things you want to *have*. It can be so delightful to discover how much your vision can support your desired way of being.

I chose many years ago to live a peaceful, compassionate, delightful, and inspiring life. I wrote that into my vision. From time to time, I still get caught up in the to-dos of life and forget about who I want to be and how I want to express myself. When I read my vision, the one sentence that leaps out at me every time and grounds me is this: "I inspire others through my delight in life."

No matter how depressed I may feel at the moment, that one line lifts me up, brings me peace, and inspires me. I begin to wonder, "Where will my delight come forth today so that I can inspire others?" As you use the exercises in this chapter to write your vision, look to see what you most want to bring forth that will inspire your sense of purpose. Write that down. Include it in your vision statement.

Creating Your Life Vision

A life vision statement can be quite short, perhaps a paragraph or two, or it can be longer, up to two pages. Its length is up to you, but I recommend keeping it short enough to read in fewer than ten minutes. A brief vision statement will be easier to read frequently and can be just as inspiring as a wordier version. You can address any area of your life to bring greater clarity. Possible topics include your career, education, or lifelong learning goals; where you want to live; the sort of people you want in your circle; and, most crucially, who you intend to be and how you want to feel.

A vision statement can vary greatly from one person to the next, depending on that individual's life circumstances. If you are a young person just finishing your formal education, you are more likely to focus on securing career work, discovering a life partner, and determining where you want to live. An older person might focus on lifelong learning goals, how they want their familial relationships to be, a vision for retirement activities, or travel plans.

Now that we've discussed some generalities of vision statements, it's time to start shaping yours. Take a few minutes right now to jot down a few things that are going well in your life. What do you like or even love about your life? Even if it seems your whole life isn't as you want it to be, usually there is some area you can feel good about. It could be that you are healthy and strong. If you do not enjoy good health, then you may have the support of your faith, live in a lovely place or have a friend you enjoy. Maybe you enjoy writing, music, rebuilding old cars, fishing and hunting, quilting, or woodworking, and the list goes on. Even if you are not actively engaged with that certain activity in your life currently, consider including it in these first notes. As you make these notes, let me share more of Matthew's story.

A Coaching Story: Matthew's Purpose and Vision

Matthew approached me to be his financial coach with a clear purpose in mind: to make a significant difference in how communities treat runaway teens and adolescents. After his experiences as a teenager living on the street and in shelters with other homeless teens, he was committed to helping young people in similar circumstances. He focused his studies in college on this cause and attained a master's degree in social work. Unfortunately, as I shared earlier, he also accrued $72,000 in student loans. He had no idea how to earn enough to pay off the loans on the wages paid by programs for runaways.

As Matthew began creating a detailed vision for the work he wanted to do and the life he wanted to live, he included his *purpose of helping runaway teens* in that vision.

That purpose had kept him focused through more than five years of college, even though he had not actually written out his vision statement. Now, considering his large debt, he needed to create a vision statement that aligned with his purpose and would inspire and motivate him during the years he would be repaying that debt (as well as into his years as an advocate, activist, and mentor). He realized he wanted to be proactive, so he set a pretty aggressive task for himself to get out of debt within five years. (Recall that a goal is an activity that moves you toward your vision, while a task clears away the obstacles to realizing your vision.) Matthew wrote some strategies to accomplish being debt-free into his vision statement. These included working a second job, looking for ways he could mindfully cut costs, such as one beer per week instead of several and sharing a house to split rent, so that he could put what he saved toward the debt.

Explore Your Vision in the Context of Peace

Look at what you've written in your vision statement so far. If you have the intention of bringing more peace into your life, does your vision statement show this? Is there anything you've included that does not support the peace-filled life you want? Recall what we've said earlier in the book: living a peace-filled life does not equate to a boring or inactive life. Some of the most adventurous people I know are filled with peace and serenity most of the time; nevertheless, they go into high-risk situations, such as medical professionals helping during an outbreak of Ebola virus, or people teaching principles of peace in Bosnia and Herzegovina during the Baltic wars.

So go ahead. Include whatever really turns you on! One of the most amazing and courageous journeys I can imagine is fulfilling a big desire while also learning to hold yourself in a state of peace and compassion. Ralph Marston, author of *The Daily Motivator*, says, "When you assume the task will be tedious, it will be. And your negative assumption makes the work that much harder. Decide instead to experience joy and fulfillment in every step you take. Love and appreciate the moment you're in, and no matter what the task may be, you'll find yourself doing it with joy."[21]

Your vision for your life serves as a path to move you forward and can act as a touchstone for your vision with money, which we'll talk about in the next chapter. Crafting your life and monetary vision so that peace is at the center ensures you a sense of peace that permeates all aspects of your life.

Peace with Money Activities

- Use the vision exercise in Lesson 9 of the *Make Peace with Money Workbook* to complete writing your vision statement. Schedule time each day for the next thirty days to read your vision, sometimes out loud. Each day, when you read it, allow yourself to revise it so it is remains authentic to the desires you truly have.

- Ask yourself: "Is this a true expression of the life I want to be living right now?"

- Your vision is meant to be a living, breathing reflection of how you want your life to be. Don't just change your vision arbitrarily for the sake of changing it. But if you read something that doesn't quite work for you, go ahead and change it. Allow your vision to expand as you expand.

Optional Activities

- Now that you have a draft of your vision, consider enhancing it by creating a vision book. Start with an album or three-ring

---

21   Ralph Marston, "Fulfillment in Every Step," *The Daily Motivator* (blog), July 21, 2018, http://greatday.com/motivate/180721.html.

binder. Some folks I know even create their vision book in Microsoft PowerPoint on their computers and turn it into a slideshow to use as their screen saver. Look for quotes from others that inspire you. Keep your eye out for photos or descriptions in publications or on the web that illustrate some aspect of your vision. Clip or print them out and put them into your book. Print out a copy of your written vision and include it in your vision book. Then review it and let it inspire your actions.

- Consider making a collage (often called a vision board) on poster board. Use inspiring clippings, words, images, and anything else that reflects your vision. Then place it where you can see it on a consistent basis. I usually put mine by my side of the bed or in the bathroom so I can see it every day.

Additional Resources

- Refer to the free *Make Peace with Money Workbook* at www.makepeacewithmoney.com, Lesson 8 and Lesson 2 for the values and purpose exercise if you haven't completed that previously. Log in with the username *makepeacewithmoney* and the password *peace42*.

- *Life Visioning: A Transformative Process for Activating Your Unique Gifts and Highest Potential* by Michael Bernard Beckwith.

- *Mastering Life's Energies*, a four-day transformational training for those who know a better world is possible and want to overcome their obstacles to move forward, provided by the Academy for Coaching Excellence: https://acecoachtraining.com/intensive.

Chapter 9
BRINGING YOUR VISION FOR YOUR MONEY ALIVE

You are not here merely to prepare to make a living. You are here to enable the world to live more amply, with greater vision, with a finer spirit of hope and achievement. You are here to enrich the world, and you impoverish yourself if you forget the errand.

—Woodrow Wilson

In addition to your life vision, which you developed in the previous chapter, why might it be valuable to have a vision specifically for your money?

Many people pursue money for the sake of wealth without anchoring that pursuit to how they actually want their life to be. Monetary wealth becomes an end in itself, rather than one of many options essential to crafting a well-rounded, fulfilling life. Bringing money into your vision means focusing on details you could miss if you look only at your life as a whole—or, for that matter, only at money as a whole.

As you develop your money vision, start by writing separate notes from your life vision. Then once you have gained some clarity about the role of money in your plans, you can incorporate your monetary vision into your life vision. This way, when you read your vision, you'll have one document to read rather than two.

An alternate way to approach this step is to examine your overall vision to see where to insert information about money.

What you *believe* about money can color your monetary vision. If you are driven by scarcity, fear, entitlement, or any other limiting belief, your vision is likely to be limited as well. When you choose spacious, fulfilling thoughts about money, even if you are at the very beginning of practicing new ways of thinking, your vision is likely to be clearer and more expansive and satisfying.

Review the work you did in chapter 5 on the power of belief. If you haven't yet, do those exercises before writing the monetary section of your vision. This will reduce your chances of including self-limiting beliefs.

Establishing a Monetary Vision

There are as many possible components to a monetary vision as there are individuals who create them. You may choose to include only a few or many, depending on where you are in your life. A young adult might include information about the monetary costs and benefits of some of the things listed in the previous chapter, such as higher education, a budding career, purchasing their first home, marrying, having children, and more. Someone nearing or at retirement age might include the costs and benefits of downsizing a home or planning for life after retiring, including travel, health, lifelong learning, and more.

Be sure to include how you want to experience your money. Do you want to feel empowered? Happy? Enriched? Generous? Excited? At ease? At peace? What else might you include in addition to, or instead of, those feelings I've listed?

If money could have any meaning in the world for you, how would you want to think, be, and act with your money? Answering the following questions will guide you in determining the meaning money has for you.

Money Inflow

- How might you want to structure your income efforts so that money works for you, rather than you working quite so hard for your money?

- What would "working smart" for your money be like? That is, can you develop passive income, start a side business, contribute more money to your savings account every month, or pursue another option to help bolster your financial health?

- Who could mentor you to work smarter if you don't yet know how?

- Similarly, if you are retired and living on a fixed income, who might you learn from concerning how to live a fulfilling life with the resources you have?

Money Outflow

- What do you most want to spend your money on that has genuine and true meaning for you rather than simply spending it willy-nilly without a vision or a plan?

- How might you want to shift your use of money so it is more satisfying to you?

- Do you currently have some discretionary expenses that do not bring you true peace and fulfillment (e.g., eating out every day or gambling or buying yet another gaming app)? If so, can you commit to reducing or eliminating these expenses?

It's beneficial to align your financial planning to the larger intentions you hold for your life. Your intentions can be in the realm of being a loving family member, being financially successful, being an effective leader, or being professionally successful. One of mine is to be an inspiring mentor. Another is to be an effective financial coach.

When I became a financial coach, it was vital to me that my money practices align with my life's intentions to be financially successful and to have a peace-filled relationship with money. I use QuickBooks, which lets me keep track of all forms of income, their source, and to which account I deposit the income. It also keeps track of every expense and whether it is personal or business. I track amounts I shift from checking accounts into savings for taxes, business savings, and personal savings. And I track our retirement investment accounts. Having certainty about my own finances allows me to be a more effective financial coach, as well.

The key is to decide what is important to you and then align your money practices with those intentions. Let's look at how you make a living. Do you already have a career, or do you want one? Do you have work that has genuine meaning for you?

Do you prefer to simply hold a job that pays the bills while you pursue a deep sense of reward in other areas of your life? David, a dear friend of mine, has a rich life outside of his work that allows him to hold a mostly mundane job without feeling deprived.

If you have a trust fund that brings you income earned by others, do you want to be a conscientious steward who demonstrates integrity and vision with that income? Who do you want to be with your money? And how can it serve you so you can serve your purpose or vision?

If you are approaching midlife, what might you want to accomplish while you are still working? Do you intend to do meaningful work even into your elder years, either paid or as a volunteer?

What do you want for your family financially as they are growing? Or for your partnered relationship? Is yours a traditional family structure? Or a creative, expanded family structure? The family structure you desire may influence what you envision for your monetary life.

While I was birthed into a somewhat traditional family with a mom, a dad, and four kids, ours was also expansively creative in that, over the years, Mom and Dad welcomed fifteen adolescents and teens that had nowhere else to live into our home. Mom and Dad both came from large families, and while they did not want to give birth to so many children, their vision included loving children and helping kids in need get to adulthood with some life skills. Without additional outside support, my parents chose to raise these youths to adulthood on their own. Mom and Dad had to build great flexibility into their household and cash flow because they never knew when another kid might need to join us.

The family I grew up in is likely not what you want as a family. However, look and see: How do you want your own family, social life, and personal support structure to be? And what kind of monetary vision goes with that?

Looking toward your elder years, how would you prefer your life to be? Healthy? Comfortable? Or something more? Wealthy? What companionship or family relations will you want? How can your monetary vision support these things? What financial planning might you want to do now in order to fulfill your vision for your elder years?

If you are already in your elder years, how might you make the most of the financial resources you have? How can you protect your resources while still having a life worth living?

I encourage you to consider where your money comes from now and where it could come from in the future. Here are some possibilities:

- a job, a career profession, or contract work
- active or passive income streams from something you create or write
- prior or future investments in stocks, bonds, or real estate
- an inheritance

Depending on what you want out of life, look for sources of income that are likely to provide security. Actions toward your money goals should stretch you but not overwhelm you.

Will you need formal education to realize your monetary vision? Or maybe you need to arrange for mentoring from someone with more experience to help you achieve your goals?

A note of caution here: a windfall, such as winning the lottery or proceeds from bets or gambling, is not predictable with any certainty whatsoever, so don't include chance winnings in your monetary vision. Your monetary vision is about that which you can actually count on yourself to generate, receive, and manage with your own effort and attention.

If you are in a love partnership, how do you want money to be between you? How might you, personally, want to think and act in order to support your vision for your partnership? How might you support your partner to fulfill his or her vision? Who will earn the income? You? Your partner? Both of you? What kind of flexibility do you personally want to bring to the partnership?

These are vital elements to keep in mind when considering your overall money vision. I've had a lot of practice managing money within a relationship after four marriages. My first marriage followed tradition in lifestyle and monetary expectations. It was also the unhappiest. I learned a lot about what not to do with money from that marriage.

My second marriage, to a good friend, rollicked through the 1970s with love, rock and roll, a lot of fun, and a lot of debt and angst. It ended in divorce, partially due to financial stress. Even so, he and I are still close friends.

During my third marriage, I pursued a stationary career while he traveled. He was a fine watercolor artist and avid outdoorsman and had the means to pursue his interests. We kept our accounts separately. Although that choice worked out well, our decision for handling our money was based on mistrust. Each of us had been married twice before and had had money problems with our spouses.

My fourth and current marriage and the joy of my life is, in many ways, quite traditional once again. We are true partners with our household money, making decisions jointly.

I am the last person to suggest that a person go through numerous relationships or marriages to learn about money. I would rather have learned my options from a mentor or coach than through so much trial and error. It's valuable to seek out education to learn about the different options you have, to discover a money structure that is workable, and that meets your individual preferences and vision. In a partnership, this means each of you will have to discover your own preferences and personal vision. Then share this information with each other.

If you start this work before you marry or make a formal romantic commitment, you'll have clearer expectations and be more likely to have a harmonious relationship. If you discover irreconcilable differences in lifestyle and your preferences about how to use money, wouldn't you rather know this before marrying? It could avoid a difficult situation where you are living with someone in disharmony that could ultimately lead to divorce.

A Coaching Story: Matthew Creates His Money Vision

Matthew had eagerly created his vision for his life and shared it with me. He already knew his purpose was to help runaway teens. He wanted to build his life around that work. Yet when I suggested that he add specifics about money to his vision, he froze, gazing at me as if I were speaking a foreign language. Here was a very smart man who had gotten the highest grades and accolades in his college studies, yet had not realized, even as he had taken on more and more debt, the impact that indebtedness would bring later. He thought he would come out of college and immediately get a good, high-paying job and start paying off the loans.

He graduated from college in 2008, just as America's Great Recession was about to hit with full force. He'd gotten in the habit of going directly from his classes to his part-time job. After work he'd go hang out with friends, then study deep into the night. He rarely looked at his financial situation because he felt so bleak about it. Adding money to his vision was a stretch for Matthew, yet once he realized the value of being completely clear about his money, he decided to tackle it head-on, like when he'd planned his coursework during college.

The first thing he wrote was an aggressive plan to pay off his $72,000 in college-related loans in five years or fewer. That meant he had to earn about $15,500 more per year than he needed for his living expenses to pay the principal and interest on the debt.

Matthew also had some important goals he wanted to accomplish during those five years. One was to climb the five highest peaks in California. Another was to take a driving trip across the country visiting cities that had the most successful programs in the nation for their teenage runaways.

To plan for these goals, Matthew had to build both time and money into his vision and then into his schedule. He had to obtain work that would give him enough income and the flexibility to do those things. Matthew saw that an important task was to live extremely frugally so he'd have resources to fulfill his other tasks and goals within his desired time frame. Because he had not obtained the nonprofit management position he'd hoped for, he had to figure out how to earn the money.

This is where the catering job Matthew had had in college came into play. Additionally, he decided to live in a communal house for a few years with four friends to further reduce living expenses. Matthew realized he was more interested in achieving his purpose and life's work than he was in how he was going to accomplish it. As long as the work was honorable and matched his values, he was willing to accept it—even if it wasn't entirely working with runaways. So he built in flexibility for how to reach his goals.

An important note: paying off his student debt was not a goal for Matthew. In the coaching model I use, goals move you specifically in the direction of your dreams or vision. Activities such as paying off debt or cleaning the garage are considered a task that, once completed, free your money, time, creativity, and energy to be directed toward fulfilling your vision and the goals that grow out of it. Matthew's goals were climbing the mountains and taking the trip across the country.

Explore Your Vision in the Context of Peace

Now that you've focused on the monetary aspect of your vision, take time to read what you've written so far and do the following:

- Answer these questions: What is missing? What can simplify or express more clearly?

- Answer this question: Which aspects of your vision involve money?

- When you write something into your vision statement, if there is a monetary cost, include how it will be met. Will it be through saving or earning a bit more just before the event? Or maybe cashing in an investment?

- Envision that each item you include in your vision statement comes about with ease. It could be as simple as, "I enjoy visiting my children, relatives, and close friends. I include the cost of these trips in my annual budget so I can travel to see them with ease."

A wonderful way to gain peace with money is to be as clear as possible about how you want to experience your money. On a separate sheet of paper, list at least three aspects or areas of your relationship with money where you are not currently at peace.

Look to see if there is something you want to include in your vision statement that will bring you greater peace with money. Often, like Matthew, this means you are willing to take on a task to clear up some debt, put a new roof on your home, or have that annual physical you've been putting off for months. All are tasks, but left unaddressed, can diminish the joy we feel as we take action toward our vision and goals.

If you don't know what to include, discuss where you are not at peace with someone who is supportive of you and your vision. If you don't have someone you can trust to support you without judgment, you may wish to consider arranging for a coaching session or meeting with your pastor or a counselor to clarify your vision for peace with money.

Peace with Money Activities

- Read over the work you've done for this chapter. What is one small step you can take right now to shift from where you are to where you want to be? Define it, then take a small action. Celebrate that you've taken this step toward greater peace.

- Take time this week to integrate the vision you've created for your money into the life vision statement you created in the previous chapter.

- If you haven't already, consider making a vision board to visually express what you've written. Here is some additional guidance for doing so:

    ◦ Look through magazines or locate images on the web that graphically express what you want. Cut them out and paste them, collage-style, to a poster board or into a journal or notebook.

- Find positive words or phrases that describe how you want to feel and what you want to accomplish with your vision. Glue those to your vision board.

- Place a photo you like of yourself somewhere in your collage so that you are also "in the picture" of your vision. If you don't have one, consider getting one made. A selfie that you print out will do just fine.

- Some people create their board electronically or photograph it and use it as a screen saver. That way you can see it every day.

- Allow your vision board to inspire you to choose at least one tiny step you'll take each day in support of your vision for your life.

Additional Resources

- Refer to the free *Make Peace with Money Workbook* at www.makepeacewithmoney.com, Lesson 9. Log in with the username *makepeacewithmoney* and the password *peace42*.

- *Life Visioning: A Transformative Process for Activating Your Unique Gifts and Highest Potential* by Michael Bernard Beckwith.

Chapter 10
CHOOSING EASE OVER STRUGGLE WITH MONEY

The most beautiful people we have known are those who have known defeat, known suffering, known struggle, known loss, and have found their way out of the depths. These persons have an appreciation, a sensitivity, and an understanding of life that fills them with compassion, gentleness, and a deep loving concern. Beautiful people do not just happen.

—Elisabeth Kubler-Ross

Those who know struggle, defeat, and suffering around money often feel they are at war with it. At the minimum, they may experience conflicted emotions about it. To them, it seems there will never be a cessation from suffering, much less any ease or peace.

And yet, as Elisabeth Kübler-Ross points out in the epigraph for this chapter, some of the dearest, most centered and peaceful people have faced severe struggles and found their way out. They have come to a place of empowerment and peace with their lives and often, too, with money. Usually, in the process, they have cultivated a vision for their lives that is deeply rewarding. And they've taken action to realize that vision.

Not only do they experience peace with money on a consistent basis, their money becomes one of the vehicles they use as a means to consciously fulfill long-held hopes and dreams.

Just because you are wrestling with money at the moment does not mean you must do so forever. Yet it takes a firm decision to change your circumstances and a commitment to act on your decision. You may need to gain some knowledge to learn how to get where you want to go. And you'll want to surround yourself with people who can be supportive of your plan.

Bringing your vision and goals into coherence with your values and the intentions you have for your life is a powerful first step to choosing ease over struggle with money. Look back at the values and purpose activities you completed in chapter 8. You can use these values and your purpose to guide you.

Next, create a series of small yet achievable action steps aimed at getting results that line up with the vision statement you created in chapter 9. For example, if your vision includes buying your next car with cash three years from now to eliminate car payments, start by determining what kind of vehicle would suit your needs and how much money you will need to save each month. This is a powerful method to reduce your discomfort and increase your sense of satisfaction and peace. Even though the steps are small, you'll be taking some specific actions toward your dreams. Affirmations, affirmative prayer, and reading your vision regularly can all support you in realizing your vision.

Beyond creating a vision that's aligned with your values and intentions, it's essential that you know exactly where you stand at this very moment with money.

You may ask, "Just how does clarity about my money relate to realizing my vision?"

When you know where you stand with money, you can see clearly what might get in the way of actually realizing your monetary vision. When you know where you stand financially, you can take action to clear up any financial problems or situations that don't enable you to reach your goals. Use the exercises in the *Make Peace with Money Workbook*, Lesson 10, to learn just where you stand with money. Upcoming chapters will guide you to more actions you can take to alter your circumstances.

When you hold a negative belief about money, those thoughts can intensify the challenges you have with it. If you believe making money is difficult, you are more likely to conduct your life in such a way that hard work for money is all you know. However, if you believe that money is merely a device to be used with skill and that you can learn that skill, you nurture a greater sense of ease.

Let's examine this atmosphere of struggle around money and what you might do to change your circumstances. Your challenges may be similar to those we talk about here, or you may endure different trials involving money. Whatever the case, it's useful to keep looking until you identify your struggles clearly. Without observing and owning challenges you experience, how can you hope to change them?

Following are a number of common factors that contribute to negative encounters people have with money. While you are reading this, consider which ones might be characteristics you exhibit. Then decide whether they affect you enough that you might be willing to change.

Spending More Than You Make

How could a person consistently overspend their income without getting into trouble financially? Yet people around the world do it regularly. The truth is that those who habitually overspend are in trouble. Some overspend by just a small amount each month. It adds up, though, and before long they realize they've gotten into serious debt. Perhaps for a while they "tighten their belts" by doing without until they get the debt paid down.

When people who have spent more than their income try to correct their course, they often go without attending to health or safety essentials, such as getting routine medical exams, replacing bald tires, or buying a new ladder to take the place of a rickety one. Some turn down the thermostat and go without heat in their home or office until they can pay off their debt. They may stop tithing or donating to causes they'd prefer to support. They eat at home rather than dining out and cut corners however they can.

Then, once their debt is paid, these individuals resume spending. Sooner or later they realize they have to go without again. What chance do you think they have, either in the spending cycle or the belt-cinching cycle, for genuine peace and happiness with money?

Others overspend by obtaining credit cards and using them instead of cash, hoping they will have more income soon to pay off the debt. Yet they haven't made a realistic plan to obtain more income. Or they overspend by making a payment toward one credit card by using another card, not realizing how much money is dribbling (or sometimes gushing) down the drain in the interest paid. This can mount to hundreds if not thousands of dollars over the course of paying off the debt.

Do you have credit card debt? Do you know the exact percentage of interest you pay each month on this unsecured debt? (Unsecured debt is a financial obligation that does not have specific property, like your house or car, serving as collateral for the value of the debt.) Many card companies charge you 15 to 21 percent or more over the course of the year on unpaid balances: if you owe $2,000, the interest alone over the course of a year could amount to $300 to $420. Wouldn't you rather spend the money you earn on something you value? Or contribute it to an organization whose work you admire?

Make note of the balance you owe on each of your credit cards. Determine the percentage of interest you are paying to each creditor. The annual statements credit cards send for your tax purposes will show exactly how much you've spent in interest for the previous year. We'll use that information later to help you begin taking some practical measures to gain greater peace with your money. In the *Make Peace with Money Workbook*, use the template in the Lesson 10 exercises to accumulate this information.

Being Less than Fully Conscious of the Consequences of Your Spending

Another scenario in which people struggle is when they are not entirely conscious about the consequences of their spending.

For example, there was a period of time in my early adulthood when, if I saw a pair of earrings I liked, I bought them without thinking. And my tastes were relatively expensive. Afterward, when I thought about my house payment or the utilities due, I'd be horrified because I wouldn't know where the money to pay those expenses was going to come from.

People who are less than fully conscious about money usually know something is out of order, yet they keep spending. Then, when the rent or house payment is due and they don't have it, they put that balance on the credit card too (or borrow it from someone). Or they get a payday-advance loan not realizing the exorbitant interest they will pay. (Such businesses often charge 15 to 30 percent or more for each loan. So, if you borrow $100, you may have to pay $115 to $130 when you pay it back.) You can learn more about the high cost of these loans at the Federal Trade Commission's website, which is listed in the Additional Resources section of this chapter.

If you have a savings account but have not been saving regularly, make note of the debt you owe to yourself. While you don't have to pay interest on such a debt, look to see the cost to your conscience of not honoring your commitment to yourself and your financial well-being.

It is much too easy to overspend your income when you don't have a grasp of how much you actually require for basic living expenses. In chapter 11, you'll determine the dollar amount you need to cover your core living expenses. You may already know this. If you do, wonderful! Pat yourself on the back. And check out the exercise in chapter 11 anyway. Many people are surprised when they learn during this exercise that there are some periodic expenses they had not thought about.

By knowing what you need and how you actually spend money (which I encourage you to track this week), you can adjust your spending so you have greater ease with your money right away and, in time, greater peace with it. If you are having trouble seeing where you can make adjustments, consider meeting with a financial coach or advisor to go over your figures with them. They often know possibilities you may not see because you are too close to your own habits.

Lacking Adequate Income

Another place people suffer is from a lack of adequate income. Consider a time when you experienced inadequate income. This may be happening right now, or perhaps it occurred in the past. For some, this is a temporary event lasting a few weeks or months or even a year or two. For others, it may be a chronic situation that's been in place most, if not all, of their adult lives.

When you lack adequate income, you may be able to cover rent but are unable to purchase healthy, nourishing food. You may have a car for transportation but you can't cover its maintenance. You may need additional professional training to better your conditions but don't know how you could afford the cost.

As with other types of financial struggles, if your income is inadequate your first step is to determine exactly what your expenses are, what your actual income is, and how much of a gap there is between them. You may need to consider cutting expenses. If you've already cut spending as much as you can, your next step is to discover how you can earn or receive more income. There is no magic bullet here.

Overcoming this particular form of struggle requires courage. It asks that you be receptive to different possibilities. It often requires looking beyond your immediate circumstances, even while you take steps to change the current situation.

You have already identified some attitudes and beliefs about money that you could change in the interest of gaining additional income in the long term. If you have read this far, you've likely already been thinking about how to change your thought patterns or have even begun working toward that change.

You may realize that you want or need to get some professional training. Or you may discover you could earn money from a skill or talent you'd dismissed as not being viable. You might decide to take on part-time work for a while in addition to your regular job. If you are self-employed, you may realize you haven't charged enough for your services and make an adjustment upward. Or you might come out of retirement to work part-time or full-time to change your circumstances.

John, a school chum of mine, worked for years as an auto mechanic. His wages were decent enough but after bills there was nothing to save for retirement. He had a hobby of working with wood. He learned there was a demand for lathe work for the restoration of historic houses and furniture. He turned his hobby into a profitable secondary stream of income and put it all into a Roth IRA fund for his retirement. His wife was supportive, as was the local woodworking group who mentored him to turn his hobby into a small business. John was able to save for retirement by doing what he loved.

To make a significant change in your situation, it is valuable— if not downright essential—to get support from others. Many people go through periods where their income is wholly inadequate. Many change their circumstances through finding mentors, pursuing additional education, and embracing the supportiveness of friends and family members. They are willing to do whatever it takes, within their values and ethics, to become stable financially.

Some of these people who've forged a new financial path are willing to act as mentors or coaches. If you were lost in the dark woods, and someone who knew the path came to you with a flashlight, wouldn't you be willing to ask for their help? Yet we allow our shame around how we've handled money to keep us from enlisting the very help that could lead us out of our most challenging circumstances. We talk more about how to enlist this kind of help in chapter 12.

Spending on Things That Don't Bring Satisfaction or Joy

Whether or not you have enough money, you may struggle because you spend your money on things that do not bring genuine satisfaction, much less joy. Have you ever gotten excited about something you were going to buy? Then you bought it and before you even got home you started to experience dissatisfaction? People who feel this discontent generally have not acted in a manner that is coherent with their values. This incoherence leads to further money struggles. You go for immediate gratification, rather than staying in touch with your long-term vision.

Consider this: Ryan is an off-road vehicle salesman. He frequently sees people who, spur-of-the-moment, purchase an off-road vehicle costing thousands of dollars. Since they haven't thought through their purchase, sometimes they default on the loan. Sometimes they bring the vehicle back after having used it and ask for their money back. Because it's been used, they take a loss. On the other hand, some buyers actually use their vehicle for good purposes and thoroughly enjoy it. It's Ryan's job to sell the off-road vehicle, yet it saddens him when people purchase quickly because, after years of selling, he can usually tell who will enjoy the vehicle and who is likely to default. Ryan says those who enjoy their purchase have planned and saved for it. It is part of their overall plan for a rewarding life.

There are ways to ensure satisfaction and even joy in how you live with your money. One way is to be clear about where you are headed. Creating a vision in Chapters 8 and 9 can help you gain that clarity. Go back and do those exercises if you haven't done so already. When your purchases are aligned with what you find meaningful, you are much more likely to be at peace with how you've used your money. You'll be in charge of your money rather than be driven by it.

Not Knowing How Much Money You Have

Some people have ample money, yet they are driven by the fear that they don't. They've never taken time to clearly examine where they stand financially. They actually do not know they have enough money because they've never defined what "enough" is. Others may genuinely not have enough money and need to make some lifestyle changes, yet they fail to take action out of fear they'll feel deprived. Meanwhile, they continue to accrue debt month by month.

Chuck, a man in his early fifties, was diagnosed with a slowly developing form of multiple sclerosis. He was terrified that he might live a long life but, unable to work, would run out of income.

Looking at his resources, we sorted out that he had modest income from a military pension and had made diverse investments that had weathered the Great Recession quite well. He earned in the high $40,000s from the job he'd had for the past twelve years. Chuck contributed 15 percent of his income to a retirement fund matched by his employer $1 to every $2 he put in. He had health insurance through his work. He would get Social Security income and Medicare at age sixty-six. And though he didn't use it, Chuck was also eligible for veteran's medical care.

He and his wife were accustomed to purchasing whatever they wanted, whenever they wanted it. They paid cash for most purchases, their home was nearly paid for, and they had relatively limited debt. If he became disabled before he was old enough to draw Social Security, he had disability insurance.

Once Chuck got clarity about exactly where he stood, which he had never done before, he and his wife made a number of adjustments in their spending and added to their retirement investments so their resources would have a greater likelihood of lasting well into their old age. Chuck was able to relax and stop worrying about money. I received a letter from his wife thanking me for coaching him to relieve his fears. She said his multiple sclerosis symptoms had decreased because he was feeling less stressed and more at peace with money, and she could relax and focus more on supporting his physical well-being.

Another couple, Ross and Ellie, both about age thirty, realized they were going deeper and deeper into debt because they weren't paying attention to their expenditures versus their income. They were scared they would not be able to support themselves adequately while taking the steps required to get out of debt. We worked out a budget that, while very frugal, was still livable.

Ross, an excellent writer when he was in college, began doing freelance technical writing on the side, adding several hundred dollars each month to their income. They applied this directly to their debt. Though they'd been eating lunch and dinner out or stopping by restaurants for takeout, they began to share meal preparation at home, which also netted them a few hundred extra dollars monthly. They put half of what they saved into a savings account for emergencies and applied the other half to their bills. Before coaching, they'd been so stressed that they weren't able to see how they might address their debt.

The more clarity Ross and Ellie gained about how much money they actually had, the more peace and freedom they began to experience with their finances. They paid their debt off entirely and grew confident enough with their finances to start the family they both wanted. About a year after their debt was retired, I talked with Ellie. She was eight months pregnant and radiant. She appreciated the improved nutrition from cooking meals at home and stated that they were keeping to their budget because they both saw how much more relaxed they were about money when they did so.

Lacking Clarity about the Money You Spend

Time and time again people approach me who have virtually no idea of the amount of money they spend in a month. Surprisingly, many also do not know the exact amount of income they bring in each month. Without a tracking system in place for receiving and spending, it is too easy to have no idea how much you earn or spend in a month, a week, or even a day.

If this is an area of struggle for you, I encourage you to begin the practice of carrying a notebook or using an app on your phone to record everything you spend. Make note each time you receive money, including the amount received. This can be your wages, interest earned, money from clients or a business, a gift, or something else. Note it down to the penny and then review what you've entered at the end of each day. Notice if there was anything spent or received that didn't get noted, then add it during your review.

Not knowing how much you spend and the income you have only creates more stress in your life. Becoming clear can show you where you leak money and where you are spending it well.

Have you ever received a bill that you didn't have enough cash to pay, yet you had no idea where your money had gone? This is direct evidence that you are unaware of your spending and not relating spending needs to your income. If you are willing, it's time to roll up your sleeves and learn what you need to know.

When you don't know how much you actually spend, then you don't know how much you reasonably *could* spend. The difference may be greater than you think. Or less. Only the facts will tell. The difference between overspending and living within your means is the difference between feeling fearful of and trapped by money and finding peace.

Just as being organized gives you more freedom with your time, so tracking your expenses will give you more freedom with your money. Wouldn't it be better to start each month knowing exactly how much you have to spend, and then see how you can spend it in a way that will bring you satisfaction, a sense of living with integrity, and a feeling of ease?

Using the tracking system of your choice, you will learn the truth of how many mocha lattes you can actually afford to buy in a week versus how many you have been buying all along. Once you get into the habit of tracking your money, you'll make better choices with how you spend it. Over time, you may begin to see this journey as the adventure it can be—and you may plan your money so it fulfills your vision for your life as abundantly as possible.

Not Knowing How Much Money You Require to Live as You Desire

You may never have taken a clear look at what you actually need to live the lifestyle you want. You get a job, make money, and spend money yet never seem to make ends meet.

Harold was a hospital pharmacist who worked long shifts filling in for pharmacists around the country. He drew a lot of overtime pay. His lodging and utilities were paid by his employers and he typically took home $70,000 to $80,000 per year after taxes. He was generous, yet traveling as much as he did, he was insecure about his likability. He gave away money to friends, family, and, frequently, total strangers. In fact, he became recognized as a soft touch and people would hit him up for money for their rent, car repairs, and more. He never knew whether people liked him or his ability to pay their bills.

When we added up Harold's actual living expenses for food, transportation, medical care, basic clothing needs, and incidentals, we found he needed just $2,250 per month to take care of those expenses with ease. That amounted to $27,000 per year. Harold was shocked to learn he had between $43,000 and $53,000 per year in spending money, which, as he astutely noted, he had been "frittering away." While he was only a few thousand dollars in debt, he had never saved money and was not in good condition for his impending retirement. So he began budgeting $500 per month to fulfill his generous spirit and saved and invested the rest. He also began to examine how he could reduce expenses after retirement and live on the approximately $2,000 per month he anticipated receiving from Social Security and income from the investments he'd make—which his adviser estimated would be about $800 per month if he was rigorous about his investment plan.

While his savings are not enough to ensure he will have enough money if he gets seriously ill or lives to an extremely old age, Harold has reduced his living expenses to about $1,800 per month by paying off his car. He decided it would be good practice learning to live within his Social Security income and hopes to continue saving between $300 and $400 per month from it after he retires. Interestingly, Harold says now he is more peaceful with his money than ever before, even though he now spends only about one-third of what he had been spending.

Harold is still generous, but consciously and intentionally so, and well within his means. Perhaps the most important outcome of our coaching was that Harold identified some causes he believed in, started to volunteer whenever he was in his hometown, and began making friends with people who did not ask him to pay their bills. This gave him a support structure for the changes he wanted to make so that he did not need to rely solely on his own motivation.

Not Having Clear Direction to Focus Actions

Significant money struggles can come when people are not clear about what they want and are too prideful or shy to ask others to help them figure it out. Imagine you are at home base on a baseball field holding a bat, expecting to hit the ball—blindfolded. Even if by some wild chance you were able to hit the ball, you'd have little to no possibility of hitting it where you wanted it to go. Imagine the ball is your money. When a person is simply muddling through life with no clear direction, it is like being blindfolded on home base.

A Coaching Story: Matthew's Practical Struggle with Money

Now let's see how this coaching approach applied to Matthew. Matthew had gone straight out of college into a job before he came to me for coaching. He had done almost no work to address his own limiting beliefs. Further, Matthew's only clear desire was to help runaway teens—yet he had no idea how he could do it while also sustaining himself financially.

College traditions are certainly time-honored, and Matthew's college experience was no exception. Although he did well with his studies, there were also many beer-filled nights, funded by a credit card he had been fortunate—or cursed, depending on your point of view—to receive during a frosh-week campus credit card push. (Spoiler alert: If you are just starting college, beware of credit card pushers. Get support to make wise decisions about funding your college and expenses. Credit cards, with their high interest rates, are not the best way.) While Matthew had held a part-time job throughout his studies, he had no tracking system, nor did he know exactly what he was spending each month. He also had no idea how much or little he was paying in interest on his cards and loans. After all, doesn't everyone go into debt to get a degree?

All these elements formed the basis of Matthew's struggle. It was relatively easy to get college loans so when he ran out of money, he simply applied for more. Though he had a purpose to get through college and work with teens thereafter, he had almost no definition of how he wanted the rest of his life outside of that work to be.

Matthew was smart enough to be aware he wasn't making the

best monetary decisions, yet he felt he was entitled to enjoy school. After all, he thought, "I'll get responsible later." "Later" was when he came to me for coaching. Matthew stated that he wished he'd gotten financial coaching before he started college. He felt he wouldn't have gone as far into debt and would have made smarter decisions about money if he'd done so.

Money spent without having a sense of purpose is money more likely to dribble away; the person spending is unlikely to have a sense of peace or satisfaction about their money. To discover more about what your aim or purpose for your money can be, read and do the exercises in chapters 8 and 9.

Peace with Money Activities

Activity One

Carry a notepad or take notes on your smartphone or tablet. Make note of exactly what you spend and when. There are a number of apps that can help with this. In addition, make note of the following:

- Are you spending money you've earned? Or are you spending money that a bank, credit card, or other creditor has loaned you?

- Observe how you feel generally when you spend money. Are you calm? At peace? Satisfied with your decisions? Or are you struggling with spending decisions?

- Observe how you feel specifically when you spend money. Do you feel anger, happiness, fear, delight, frustration, satisfaction, a sense of unease, or something else?

- If you said something about yourself in regard to money

while you spent it, note that. Examples include the following:

- ◦ "That was stupid."
- ◦ "This actually supports my vision!"
- ◦ "I'm sure bad with money."
- ◦ "Great. That's in my budget."
- ◦ "No one will ever know I overspent."

- After several days, review your notes for any patterns. Particularly, notice times you felt a sense of satisfaction, ease, or peace with financial decisions. This gives you a place to start in building your own peace with money. Record these notes for at least seven days.

Activity Two

Use the worksheet in Lesson 10 of the *Make Peace with Money Workbook* to list your debt and the interest you are paying. Include what you promised yourself that you would save for the past month if you have not been honoring your saving commitment. This could be either money put into a "rainy-day" account to cover auto, veterinarian, or other periodic expenses or a sunshine-opportunity account where you save for a class to learn something new, to go on vacation, or to buy gifts for yourself or those you love. Or both.

Additional Resources

- Refer to the free *Make Peace with Money Workbook* at www.makepeacewithmoney.com, Lesson 10. Log in with the username *makepeacewithmoney* and the password *peace42*.
- *Money: Master the Game* by Tony Robbins.

- *The Energy of Money* by Maria Nemeth, the forgiveness process, pages 210–217.

- "Payday Loans" on the Federal Trade Commission's website: https://www.consumer.ftc.gov/articles/0097-payday-loans.

Chapter 11
PEACE INCREASES WITH CERTAINTY

It's the little details that are vital.
Little things make big things happen.

—John Wooden

You spend much of your time wishing things were different. Yet you spend little time changing your thoughts and taking actions to make things different. If this is your scenario, it is likely you will spend your whole life wishing for fulfillment rather than being fulfilled.

Much of the pain people experience about money comes from uncertainty, from worrying or wishing. In this chapter, you'll gain certainty about where your money comes from and where it goes.

Some people like what they see when they do the work of this chapter. Others become quite uncomfortable. Yet they are willing to acknowledge and tell the truth about their monetary situation. They realize learning about their own situation propels them toward having a more fruitful relationship with money.

Knowing your numbers is an empowering step. Once you know where you stand, you can begin taking small yet attainable steps toward changing what doesn't work for you. You'll see the power of aligning your finances to the life you want to live. As you let go of old patterns and inhibiting thoughts and conclusions you have about money, greater peace naturally follows.

Usually, when people decide to change their relationship with money, they plot out exactly how much income they have and how much they owe. For many, clarity about this can be scary. Some see that they owe more than they can reasonably repay and still maintain the standard of living they desire. Some are fearful their money will run out before the end of their lives. Many know they should keep better track of spending or keep their checking account balanced—but going shopping is so much more fun!

Often people vow to handle their money responsibly for a while but have little motivation to keep it up long term. This is usually because their decision is not anchored to a vision that has substance. When there's no motivation, tending to money matters may not seem relevant.

Yet isn't keeping track of your money day-to-day equally as useful as all the other money-wise choices, such as staying mindful with money, developing a positive and affirming relationship with it, and getting support when you don't know something you need to know about finances? The short answer, of course, is yes. Even so, you'll notice we haven't addressed money details fully until now.

Think about this: You already feel challenged about money. Some relative says, "You must balance your checkbook to the penny so you always know where you stand with money." Or your banker says, "You should get a snapshot of your net worth." So you begin working on your financial record keeping. Perhaps you don't feel very skilled at it. And when you see the money details emerging, you may begin feeling even more pain. At some point you'll stop attending to details and go back to doing it the way you always have.

I hope by now you have developed a clear vision of what you want for your life and your financial well-being. I also hope you're willing to do whatever it takes to help yourself shift to a healthier relationship with money.

In this chapter, you'll work with the *Make Peace with Money Workbook* to get a Money Snapshot, also known as your net worth statement. Essentially, this is what you own minus what you owe at a specific point in time. You may have a positive net worth or a negative net worth. In other words, you may have monetary value and ownership greater than you owe. Or, conversely, you may owe more than you own. You will also see how your income matches up with your expenses. Do you earn more than you spend? Or do you spend more than you earn?

I encourage you to make note of your spending to the penny for a week (or longer if you have the will and courage to do it). You'll see where you are spending money in ways that don't support the vision you have for your life. When you spend consistently outside your values and the plans you have for your life, this is called leaking money. Tracking spending helps you see where you are leaking money in small or large amounts. It is amazing how quickly these leaks can add up.

People often leak money with the interest they pay on unsecured debt, also known as credit card debt or unsecured loans. The interest you pay on this kind of debt is higher (often much higher) than debt you owe on a secured loan, such as a mortgage or auto loan. When you examine your financial situation, you may realize you have unsecured debt. This is your chance to plan for paying off this debt, so the energy you put into making money goes more fully toward supporting your vision rather than paying off debt and interest charges.

A Money Snapshot: Your Net Worth

A vital starting point in the practical journey toward making peace with money is to determine exactly what your current financial situation is. This is a picture of exactly where you stand financially at a given moment in time. This clear, foundational information can inform future financial decisions, such as what to invest in, how to spend your money, or how to grow your business.

The process of taking this Money Snapshot usually brings up some feelings. You may feel anxious or worried that you don't know how to do it. Or you may not want to see what is actually true about your money. The first time I did this, I realized my net worth was in the negative by nearly $15,000. It spurred me to make changes toward having a positive net worth. Now, nearly thirty years later, I have such a positive net worth that I know I can retire in a couple of years and be financially stable, likely for the rest of my life.

Even if you don't particularly want to look at your net worth, I encourage you to ask yourself, "Am I willing to do this in the interest of greater well-being with my money?" Your answer initially may be a resounding no. If that is the case, notice whether you'll have greater discomfort in the long run if you don't take this step. In other words, are you likely to be prolonging your financial pain and struggles by not doing it? Now ask yourself again, "Am I willing?"

If you have a bookkeeper or an accountant, they can help you determine your net worth. There are freelance bookkeepers who work at an hourly fee to help with this if you desire. The Money Snapshot worksheet in Lesson 11 of the *Make Peace with Money*

Workbook is designed to support you in compiling this information for yourself.

Your net worth statement includes the following elements:

- The exact amount you have in checking, savings, and insurance and investment accounts on a given day.

- The value of what you own outright with no loans or liens (such as vehicles, machinery, tools, jewelry, artwork, collectibles, and more), valued at what you could actually get if you were to sell them now.

- Real estate, based on the appraised value of the property, minus any loans or liens you have against the appraised value.

- The total of the preceding items minus the amount you owe in loans, credit card balances, and other debts or liens.

Budgeting and Peace

Once you determine your net worth and have the clarity a Money Snapshot gives you, you can then turn to creating an empowered budget. A budget is your financial road map. When used well, it supports your financial health and contributes to your peace of mind.

I define a budget as: *A plan for getting money (your income) and spending money (your expenses) to reach identified goals by a specific time.*

Budgets typically cover a full year, although breaking the budget down into a monthly budget can help you manage your money month by month. It's useful, when creating your annual budget, to realize that some expenses, like your house payment, utilities, food and more, come around every month, while other expenses are periodic, perhaps quarterly or annual.

Examples of periodic expenses include taxes; auto, home, health, and life insurance; medical and dental checkups; annual charitable donations; veterinarian bills for pets; magazine subscriptions and membership dues; and auto maintenance, among others. By finding out how much you spend each year on these, you can plan an amount to set aside each month into savings, so you have the required funds when each payment is due.

If you wish to add to your longer-term peace with money, begin to plan for retirement if you have not already done so. If you are in your fifties or sixties, you may feel it's too late. Please don't. I've worked with numerous people who have created a plan even in their mid-sixties. They have stuck with it and it has brought them greater financial security, and therefore a greater sense of calm and peace. If you plan to set aside some form of investments or savings, you'll want to work with a financial coach or retirement planner to look at your options and help you decide what is most workable for you.

To create your budget, turn to the exercises and tools in Lesson 11 in the *Make Peace with Money Workbook* and use the Budget Worksheet. I've included a sample budget so if you are unfamiliar with budgeting you'll have an example to work with. Enter income sources and all of your monthly, annual, and periodic expenses. You'll be able to adjust amounts you plan to spend. You can determine if your income exceeds your expenses or whether you have a shortage. Use your budget and your net worth statement in tandem to plan how you can build more ease into your monetary life.

You may say, "Coach, of course I want to have more ease with money, but right now this is hard work!"

Most people I coach feel this way at some point during the process. Think about this: if you were practicing to be a marathon runner, concert pianist, yoga teacher or professional chef, you would almost certainly encounter times when you wondered why on earth you chose that course of action because it feels so difficult.

To become proficient at anything takes learning what you need to know, being willing to learn from others who have the skills you want to master, and lots of practice. Learning to be masterful with your money is no different.

As you learn, you may see you need to decrease your expenses. The "Activity One" exercise in chapter 10 where you tracked what you actually spent in a week can help you see where you are leaking money and where you could reduce costs. You may decide you want to increase your income. If that is the case, then your budget can help you discover how much more you need to bring in. This way, you can target that amount and plan for it directly.

One reason people get into difficulty is because they are not specific about what is actually required to live within their means. Instead, they get scared or worried and spend their time in pain rather than clarity. Before we talk about tracking what you actually spend, let's check in with Matthew's story.

A Coaching Story: Matthew Counts His Money

As Matthew sought to make sense of the step discussed in this chapter, I asked him to examine his current income and spending requirements for his Money Snapshot. I helped him prepare his net worth statement so he could see exactly how much he owned and how much he owed.

Matthew got a clear picture of his real financial situation. He discovered that the value of what he owned, including his used car (which he owned free and clear) and the money in his checking and savings accounts came to $2,650. You may notice that while he owned his car, that was not liquid cash and it was necessary for his transportation to his work. His credit card debt was $18,440 and his school loans amounted to $55,560. He also had three small personal loans from friends totaling $1,245. The average percentage of interest on the credit cards was 15.9 percent. The average interest on the college loans was 3.76 percent.

Relying on this information, Matthew determined to pay off the credit card debt first so he could stop leaking money from the higher interest. Until the cards were paid off, he would pay minimum payments on the college loans. Once the cards were cleared, he would then turn to paying larger payments on the college loans.

We looked at a number of options for how he could begin addressing the debt he owed and still do the work with youth that he was so passionate about. Matthew had partially supported his way through college as an on-call waiter at a lively local diner where tips were generous. He often filled shifts while other waiters were on vacation or not available. He'd also done some banquet wait service and was very good at it.

Matthew started calling around to his contacts in that field and soon was offered a job as a banquet captain, managing high-end banquet sites on the day of the event. He worked in catering an average of three days a week. Because it was the lowest-level management, it offered a better hourly wage than waiting tables and he still got a portion of the tips, which added significantly to his income.

Then the local youth shelter offered to hire Matthew to run night patrols three nights a week to engage kids to come in from the streets. The hours were flexible, which was good because the catering work was not on a steady schedule. He didn't earn as much hourly as he did with the catering, yet Matthew realized that if he was very frugal, the shelter income would be enough for him to live on. So he chose to put 80 to 90 percent of his catering income toward the debt and the remainder into savings for any emergencies that might arise.

Matthew installed an app on his smartphone and began tracking his spending and income each day so he could see where he was leaking money on things he didn't actually need. He was appalled to discover that he was spending nearly $40 a week on beer with his buddies. Because it was only $3 a glass, it seemed so miniscule he'd never added it up. He decided to go out with the guys just once a week for a single beer. This freed up a bit more than $140 each month that he could use to pay off debt. Over the five years during which he planned to pay off the debt, that added up to $8,400. That meant he could pay off the debt in fewer than four and a half years rather than five if he stuck with his plan.

Matthew realized that for the time being he wouldn't have much of a social life due to this frugal lifestyle, but he also knew he'd be pursuing his passion of helping teens while still paying down debt at a substantial rate.

Two other areas Matthew discovered he was leaking money was in buying basketball tickets and going out to movies and buying popcorn once a week. Again, he did not fully deprive himself but decided to go to the movies once a month instead and to mostly watch the games on his tablet, attending only the occasional live event. This saved him another $130 per month, which he also put toward the debt or into savings.

Tracking What You Spend

You can see from Matthew's story that tracking what you are actually spending can reveal ways in which you may be letting money slip through your fingers. Often it's not the $50 basketball ticket but something small, yet frequent, such as a designer coffee or a couple of beers a few times a week. This can be especially true if you give yourself a cash allotment each week with no guidance as to how to use it. Many people simply go to the ATM and get cash whenever they've spent what's in their wallet. They don't attend to whether their purchases have real purpose toward the life they'd prefer to be living.

Taking practical steps can be challenging at first, but if you work through this book and the workbook step-by-step, you will see your situation with clarity and truth. You don't need to be an accounting whiz to pick up basics for tracking spending, paying down debt, or managing your bills.

For many of my clients, Matthew included, knowing their numbers and then acting from that knowledge has indeed brought about a feeling of empowerment and significant peace with money. They struggle less, and even when unexpected expenses come up, they have more resilience to address them. They feel clear and calm, and have a consistent and peaceful relationship with their money.

Peace with Money Activities

- Create your Money Snapshot. Use the worksheet in the *Make Peace with Money Workbook*, Lesson 11. This part of making peace with money takes courage and a willing heart to look at exactly where you stand at this moment financially. Use the principles you've already learned to bring calm into this process. Use your breathing. Use positive affirmations. Take a moment to remember who you want to be—a peace-filled person—even as you are doing this work.

- Track your money for one week in a notebook or app. Mint is an app that is quite easy to use and has a number of empowering applications to help you manage your money. Before using this or any money management app, I recommend you research the risk versus benefits and then determine if the app is appropriate for your needs. Risks and benefits can include the security (or not) of the app, how difficult or easy it is to use, its cost, and whether it syncs with your bank account in real time so every transaction is captured. Because information changes so quickly in the world of apps, I refer you to Consumer Reports, which regularly does reports on software and apps. Their web site is: www.consumerreports.org. Then search for "financial management apps."

- Empower yourself with a budget. Use the Budget Worksheet in Lesson 11 in the *Make Peace with Money Workbook* to create a budget, recalling that a budget is a working document. The more you use it to stay in alignment with your values and the intentions you have for your life, the more it can support your peace with money.

Additional Resources

- Refer to the free *Make Peace with Money Workbook* at www.makepeacewithmoney.com, Lesson 11. Log in with the username *makepeacewithmoney* and the password *peace42*.

- *Degunking Your Personal Finances* by Shannon Plate. This book gives clear guidance for untangling finances, with a wonderful sense of humor about it all.

Chapter 12
WHO IS YOUR TEAM?

You can do irrefutably impossible things with the right amount of planning and support from intelligent and hardworking people and pizza.

—Scott M. Gimple

Another powerful choice you can make on your financial journey is to get sound advice and support from others. Often asking for support from others, especially strangers, can range from quite uncomfortable to excruciatingly difficult.

If this is true for you, you are not alone. Many of us are uncomfortable in such a situation. Asking for information or relying on support from others about finances can feel unsafe. Doing it alone in regard to handling money has become more the norm than the exception. Yet there can be a high cost in this fierce independence so many of us demonstrate.

Decisions about money can be a lot easier when you seek out others to teach you the things you don't know yet. There are many ways you can gain support from others while addressing your monetary challenges. Support could be working with a bookkeeper, an accountant, a financial coach, a consultant, or another financial professional. Or it might be meeting with a friend twice a month to pay bills together. Or it could be asking your banker to help you balance your account statement.

Support from others to keep accurate track of your money and to address your money leaks can make your journey so much easier. One group of young women I coached a few years ago chose to get together every two weeks to get their account information up-to-date, share investment strategies, and simply know they were not alone in managing their money. Once they got used to sharing, they were able to relax and actually began having fun around living healthily with their money.

When you feel discouraged, defeated, or otherwise at odds with your money, it can be difficult to get in touch with what you want. You may simply not believe anything other than the status quo is possible. If so, this is a good place from which to seek support from a coach or other financial professional. They are trained to encourage and support you while you work through your limiting thoughts and behaviors. You'll begin to discover things you may not have known, and they'll help you build a healthier relationship with money. They will also help you see and celebrate what you are already doing well with your money.

If you are in college, on-campus services are often available. If you're over fifty (or in some places, fifty-five), generally your community's senior center can put you in touch with someone who can help. These centers may also have classes where you can expand your knowledge about finances, including budgeting on a retirement income. If you are an entrepreneur with a business, your local Small Business Development Center can often help.[22]

A coach or other professional will help you discover possibilities for changing behaviors or beliefs that are getting in your

---

22 Small Business Development Centers are under the national US Small Business Administration. You can learn more at www.sba.gov/tools/local-assistance/sbdc.

way that you may not yet see, all while guiding you through addressing your financial situation and getting in touch with a vision for your life. Let's look in greater depth at some professionals you might approach for support.

A Financial Coach

There are numerous kinds of coaching. It's helpful to know the differences so you can find the coach who can meet your current needs.

A Certified Financial Coach™, which is what I am, is a person who is trained by a financial coach–training program to help you transform your relationship with money and other forms of wealth. We show you ways to improve your financial standing so you can find clarity, peace, and ease with money, now and in the future. We help you look at the role money plays in the scope of your life as a whole. And we help you bring forth solutions and strategies to succeed in your financial life.

When you are working with something that has as much impact on our lives as money, being sure you're working with a qualified expert makes a lot of sense. Be aware that there is a difference between a prosperity coach, who will support your efforts to manifest your good, and a financial coach, who will help you address your money challenges now, so you can open a clearer pathway to prosperity.

The International Coach Federation, (see the resources at the end of this chapter for their website), can help you locate a certified coach who is qualified. Some people that promote themselves as financial coaches do not have adequate training, so I encourage you to seek out a coach who has undergone training specific to financial coaching.

Life coaches, differentiated from financial coaches, provide an ongoing partnership designed to help clients produce fulfilling results in their lives overall. Most certified financial coaches also have significant life-coach training. Most coaches with other specialties (such as physical fitness or career fields) are not trained to work with money challenges and may shy away from financial issues.

Cheaper is not always better when it comes to getting support, especially if you want to become clear, exactly and precisely, about where you are with your money. It is also not necessary to hire the most expensive person, thinking that he or she must be better because sessions cost more. It's valuable to seek support from a professional who works with people whose money challenges are similar to your own.

Financial Professionals and How They Can Benefit You

Some other financial professionals you may want to engage include the following:

- **Bookkeeper:** A bookkeeper records financial transactions for a business or individual as part of their financial record-keeping process. Individuals can usually do their own bookkeeping; however, if your books become complex, a bookkeeper can free your time to do what you do best. Transactions include payments, purchases, sales, receipts, and invoicing by an individual or business.

- **Accountant:** An accountant keeps more financial records of a person or a business and usually costs more than a bookkeeper. With clarity, you can make decisions about what is profitable, what is not, where and when to invest, how much to reserve for taxes, emergencies, and more. An accountant can help plan and forecast cash flow, make sound budgets, and estimate business and tax costs.

- **Certified Public Accountant (CPA):** A CPA is an accountant who has met education and exam requirements as defined by state law to be certified. Many small businesses contract with an independent CPA to handle accounting needs because they do not have enough work for a full-time employee. CPAs can do audits of business financial records.

- **Tax Accountant:** A tax accountant is a CPA who has been trained and specializes in the management of accounting practices involving taxes and tax laws. This type of accounting is regulated by the Internal Revenue Service.

- **Auditor:** An auditor is a person appointed and authorized to examine financial accounts, compare the charges with the vouchers, verify balance sheet and income items, and state the result. Periodic audits, usually annually, are essential for the financial health of businesses.

- **Business Consultants and Advisers:** Business consultants and advisers provide consulting to improve business performance, primarily through analysis of existing business problems. They help develop plans for improvement.

- **Business Coaches:** Business coaches provide support, training, and occasional advice to improve business effectiveness. Coaching can build leadership and improve teamwork, sales, employee accountability, and communication through strategic planning, defining goals, and more.

- **Contract Help:** This is typically short-term or occasional help hired to fill a role with a specific project or at specific times of year when the business workload requires extra help.

- **Financial Adviser:** A financial adviser is a person who is employed to provide financial services or guidance to clients. Some sell products for specific financial or investment companies and will want to sell you their products. Do your homework to determine if you will get unbiased advice from whomever you hire.

- **Broker:** A broker is an individual paid a commission for carrying out their customer's orders. They often act as an intermediary between a buyer and seller. Brokers specializing in stocks, bonds, commodities, and options act as agents and must be registered with the exchange where they do business on your behalf.

If you've never learned the basics of good money management, support is even more crucial. You'll want someone to teach and guide you, to provide accountability and support while you gain financial skills. This is the path I took when I hired my financial coach. As you learn skills and define your purpose and discover where you stand with money right now, you'll begin to see changes you want or need to make. This may include working with one or more of the other kinds of financial specialists I've listed.

I encourage you to become fully engaged with what you want to be doing in the world. This can be as simple, yet essential, as coming home to your family and kicking a soccer ball around with the kids, or it can be as expansive as a visionary desire to end world hunger or stop human trafficking. Each is equally valid because people who are at ease in their lives contribute from their well-being, whether to their family, community, or world.

A Coaching Story: Matthew's Success

By participating actively in coaching, Matthew created a clear, specific plan with measurable goals. Then he set himself into action. About two years after his coaching ended, I bumped into Matthew at a catered gala event. It would be his last event as a banquet captain in the West Coast city where he lived. He shared that a major donor to the shelter had realized what a clear spokesperson Matthew was for runaway youth and offered to fund a position to advocate for youth in Washington, DC. Part of Matthew's new work would be to meet with political leaders and "sell" them on the need to provide services for runaway and at-risk youth. Matthew felt the offer from the donor was a miracle and a dream come true. Yet I could see that the opportunity came about because of his clarity, focus, and his intentional actions to realize his vision. I recommended he study *The Soul of Selling: How to Achieve Extraordinary Results with Remarkable Ease* by Carol Costello, an innovative and personable approach to engaging others, whether for sales, advocacy, or offering a coherent point of view for others to consider.

The income from the advocacy position would be enough to replace both the catering income and his shelter work so he could continue to pay down his debt. Matthew now works full-time to create policy change and gain support at the national level for his cause. He also does shelter work part-time, which continues to fulfill his heart's desire.

At the beginning, Matthew couldn't see how it would work out to both follow his dream and pay off his debt, but by writing out his plans clearly and beginning to take steps in the direction of his goals, he's actually well along the road. He said he owed just a little over $34,000—less than half of what he owed when he graduated. He paid that much in just under two and a half years. With frugal living and clear focus on his target, Matthew estimated he would pay off the rest of the loans within twenty-eight months. This is a bit under the five-year goal he'd set for himself.

A second miracle occurred while Matthew was researching exactly what he owed on the debt and the interest he was paying. Because he worked for a nonprofit organization operating in his field of study, 10 percent of his debt was forgiven after he had worked at the shelter for two years. He no longer felt so burdened by the debt. Blessedly, he was also pursuing his dream profession. He looked forward to the day in the not-too-distant future when he and his fiancée could afford to marry, buy a home, and begin their family.

Support of Family and Friends

Don't overlook the support you can gain from family and friends who encourage your life goals. While some won't understand what you are trying to do and might not be supportive, some may well become your best champions. Be sure to acknowledge and appreciate what others do for you as you go along. And celebrate with them when one of your significant milestones is reached.

However support shows up for you, it is incredibly helpful to seek it out and allow yourself to receive it.

The value of community is often overlooked, and having a knowledgeable cheering squad behind you can make a world of difference. Whether you find a financial coach, work with another type of financial professional, or create a group of peers who are facing similar challenges to support one another, don't do this work alone.

Self-Coaching Questions

As you prepare to finish this book and pursue peace with money, ask yourself the following questions (both now and as you progress on your financial journey):

- What would it take for me to be at ease with asking for help with my finances?

- What might happen if I don't seek help? (Write down the consequences of not seeking support.)

- Am I willing, even in the face of discomfort, to seek and receive support so I can get to where I want to be with money?

Remember, some individuals need to say no to the preceding questions before they can get an authentic yes. The yes comes when they encounter yet another painful money experience and decide that support could help. Answer the self-coaching questions honestly and seek support soon.

Peace with Money Activities

- In what areas related to your money would it be useful to have support?

- What kind of support do you want?

- Are you willing to identify two or three people you can ask for support or mentoring?

- Email, text, or call one person and schedule a time to meet within one week or less.

Additional Resources

- Refer to the free *Make Peace with Money Workbook* at www.makepeacewithmoney.com, Lesson 12. Log in with the username *makepeacewithmoney* and the password *peace42*.

- International Coach Federation (www.coachfederation.org): An international organization that sets standards for the field of coaching and provides referrals to certified coaches. You can search by the type of coach you want.

- Academy for Coaching Excellence (www.acecoachtraining. com): Click on "About," then "Our Community," then "Certified Coaches" to search for coaches by region.

- *The Soul of Selling: How to Achieve Extraordinary Results with Remarkable Ease* by Carol Costello (see also www.soulof-selling.com and www.carolcostello.net)

Chapter 13
CELEBRATE!

Last year I gave myself one hundred and eight celebrations—besides the ones they close school for. I cannot get by with just a few.

—Byrd Baylor

By this point in your journey, if you have been working through the exercises in this book and the workbook, you may notice that your ability to feel at peace with money is growing. Let's now turn our attention to one more vital element to this way of being: celebration.

Your willingness to celebrate the successes you experience acknowledges your progress in your money adventure and can also inspire those around you.

When you allow others to recognize and celebrate your achievements with you, it fuels your ability to stick to your path with greater energy. You may find yourself looking for others' successes so you can celebrate with them. You may find yourself in a cycle of appreciation, gratitude, and celebration.

Making peace with money includes celebrating your relationship with money and paying attention to just how far you've come. If you've committed to change your thinking and behavior and if you follow through consistently on activities that foster peace with money, you will have accomplished significant change.

We focus so hard on changing and growing, yet rarely do we take the time to celebrate the changes that occur. In this chapter, I emphasize the value of celebration and encourage you to build celebratory practices into your life.

Gratitude is pivotal to building the energy to sustain your changes. We've already embraced gratitude as an instrument for gaining peace with money. We'll go into it even deeper here.

Wallace Wattles, in *The Science of Getting Rich*, wrote, "Many people who order their lives rightly in all other ways are kept in poverty by their lack of gratitude."[23] Sometimes the poverty is actually not having enough. All too often, though, it shows up as poverty consciousness—the feeling of never having enough even when we actually do—and the complaints that go with that frame of mind.

Gratitude and complaints cannot take up the same space. Complaints tend to generate more complaints, which can lead to feeling miserable because that is where your focus is. Gratitude, even in the midst of a challenging situation, opens your mind to seek creative solutions. When you are grateful, it's natural to want to resolve whatever is not right.

When you focus intently on your growth by learning new possibilities and changing old habits, acknowledgment of any change, no matter how small, can help you stay encouraged, even inspired.

Robert Maurer, in *One Small Step Can Change Your Life: The Kaizen Way*, says, "By taking steps so tiny that they seem trivial or even laughable, you'll sail calmly past obstacles that have defeated you before. Slowly—but painlessly!—you'll cultivate an appetite

---

23 Wallace Wattles, *The Science of Getting Rich* (n.p.: First Start Publishing e-edition, 2012), 33.

for continued success and lay down a permanent new route to change."[24]

In other words, when you recognize how much progress you've made, you gain momentum. Even if you feel frustrated, if celebration seems a stretch too far, simply acknowledging that you are advancing toward your goals can keep you inspired.

Many of us grew up in a system that gave us gold stars for achievements. Yet the essential aspect of recognizing and valuing our progress falls by the wayside as we grow up. If you don't already celebrate your accomplishments, by yourself or with others, it's never too late to start.

Perhaps your family is already committed to celebration. If that is the case, congratulations and enjoy! Many feel that to appreciate themselves for taking steps to change and grow is egotistical. I encourage you, wherever you stand on this spectrum—from feeling shy about celebration, to feeling it's ego-driven, to feeling it's a healthy and natural part of life—incorporate recognition into your daily life. You'll increase your sense of wholesomeness, plenitude, and abundance.

Beyond the simple act of recognition lies the playing field of celebration. Recognizing your achievements and then celebrating them is a proven way to bolster confidence and self-esteem.

Whenever you embark on a course of great change, although you may feel exhilaration because you've begun, you may also feel somewhat shaky or scared. Change may seem to happen only in tiny increments. The Chinese philosopher Confucius is thought

---

24   Robert Maurer, *One Small Step Can Change Your Life: The Kaizen Way* (New York: Workman, 2014), 113.

to have said, "The man who moves a mountain begins by carrying away small stones." Stay attuned to your changes as they occur.

"Celebration" is a big and joyous word, but celebration itself doesn't always have to be a big to-do. Celebration can be as simple as allowing feelings of contentment and gratitude wash over you and relishing these feelings.

If you are uncomfortable sharing with others about your new way of being with money, that's okay. But don't let this keep you from acknowledging to yourself the progress you've made. If you decide to share about your successful financial shifts with family or friends, choose those who are likely to be genuinely supportive of what this means to you. Sharing your successes allows those around you to appreciate what you are up to. The more you recognize and celebrate your successes, particularly in the company of others, the more you allow them to join with you and the more likely you are to inspire others to do the same.

If you've been doing this financial work with a partner who is reading the book and doing the activities with you, then you have a built-in celebration partner when each of you achieves your milestones. There are lots of ways to celebrate, so stay creative!

A friend of mine holds a "Celebration Sunday" once a month, where a group of friends and colleagues gather for a potluck meal. Over lunch or dinner, they share the things they are celebrating that month. This is a lovely way to strengthen the muscle of celebration. Celebrating in community adds even more inspiration because you'll give one another ideas you can act on during the following month.

Just as acknowledgment of your progress opens the flow of appreciation, it can also open the flow of abundance and prosperity.

So, what is your celebration? How far have you come? Even a seemingly tiny step can lead to big results in the long run.

If you create a new system for keeping better track of your finances, you have reason to celebrate. If you gain valuable insight that leads you to be more at ease with money, you have reason to celebrate. Be grateful for those who help with your journey, for what you learn to support your growth, for the different decisions and changes you are making, for the ability to be who you are, and for the chance to celebrate yourself and others.

Celebrating a Milestone

Betty was in quite a lot of debt when we started working together. She said, "I can't afford to hire you, but I also see I can't afford not to, since I'm not making the changes I need to make on my own."

She cut up her credit cards and committed to not creating more debt. She set a goal to pay down her debt at 5 percent of the debt principal plus the total interest that was charged for that month. This meant that, if she stayed to her plan, she would be out of debt in twenty months. To do this, she realized she would need a second job. She obtained part-time work as a file clerk, organizing and filing for a local entrepreneur on Saturdays for five hours. She was grateful for the work, but this is what she really celebrated at the end of the first month: making that first payment of 5 percent of the debt plus that month's interest.

At the end of five months, when she'd paid down the debt by 25 percent, she celebrated again. Betty celebrated each time she paid off another 25 percent. She chose very low-cost celebrations so that she wouldn't add to her debt. When the debt was fully paid, she took one month's income from her extra job to treat herself and a friend to a personal-growth course they had long wanted to attend.

I saw her six months after the debt was paid. She'd continued working at the filing job and, having paid off her debt, she'd started a savings account. She looked luminous when she told me of the vacation cruise to Costa Rica she planned to take with it. The vacation would be fully paid for up front. It was her first real vacation in more than five years.

How you celebrate is entirely up to you, according to your preferences and lifestyle. Two celebrations I love are arranging flowers into lovely bouquets, and driving to the mountains nearby to spend a day in the high country. A friend of mine celebrates by spending a day in her rose garden, deadheading her roses. Sounds like work to me, yet she loves it. It's all a matter of perspective. A male friend I went to high school with celebrates by taking a ride along California's coastal highway on his motorcycle.

A key is to realize that while celebrations can cost money, they don't have to. Another of my friends often celebrates progress he's made toward his goals with a cup of coffee and a walk on our waterfront, enjoying the beauty of the bay and the marina.

Celebrate progress by acknowledging successes in your money adventure. You may inspire others to take steps toward their own financial well-being. Making peace with money, beyond the fundamentals of managing your money well, includes celebrating your relationship with it. Allow yourself to revel, play, enjoy, and be merry—each and every step of the way.

Peace with Money Activities

- Schedule a celebration into your calendar. You can choose any milestone that feels right for you. Examples of milestones include the following:

    ◦ Noticing that you have gone one full week without incurring additional debt.

    ◦ Paying your bills in a relaxed and mindful manner.

    ◦ Reading your vision and an affirmation every day for a month.

    ◦ Completing a project you've wanted to get out of the way yet never seemed to get around to doing.

- You can celebrate alone or with others. This is about building your muscle for recognition, acknowledgment, and celebration.

- If you haven't started a gratitude journal, do so now, and keep it for at least thirty days. Consider writing down your gratitude for an even longer period of time to fully feel the benefit of this form of self-recognition.

Additional Resources

- Refer to the free *Make Peace with Money Workbook* at www.makepeacewithmoney.com, Lesson 13. Log in with the username *makepeacewithmoney* and the password *peace42*.

- *The Gratitude Diaries: How a Year Looking on the Bright Side Can Transform Your Life* by Janice Kaplan.

- *The Simple Abundance Journal of Gratitude* by Sara Ban Breathnach.

Chapter 14

UPPING THE ANTE: MAKING PEACE IN THE WORLD

I long to accomplish a great and noble task;
but it is my chief duty and joy to accomplish humble tasks
as though they were great and noble.

—Helen Keller

The practice of peace in a single area of your life—in your relationships, in the workplace, or, of course, with money—only serves to strengthen your peace practice in all areas.

Will there be faltering steps along the way? Yes, more than likely. Yet those who are successful face their challenges and come out the other side with greater resilience and peace around money. They choose a path, state it clearly, and then do what they said they would do.

I appeal to you to up your ante in an even more substantial way: to be moved with compassion for the sake of peace overall. I call on you to lean into what it looks like for you to embody peace—with money and in your life as a whole—to connect your beliefs and hopes to practical actions. And to do so in light of all that is precious and dear to you.

This could be taking a stand for peace with just one other person. Perhaps it is bringing peace into a troubled working relationship.

For many, it is a desire to make a difference toward peace and justice in what is presently unfolding in the world. Yet to be a force in these other arenas, we must also address what is not peaceful within ourselves.

Look to see what it means to step outside your comfort zone and take action that, although may be a great challenge, can also be enormously rewarding. It is less important that you carry out an agenda as an advocate for peace than it is that you faithfully lean into the value of peace, acting in such a way that your beliefs are demonstrated through all you are and all you do.

In this expanded practice of peace we are called to bring love and peace to ourselves, to our family, our neighbors, and even our adversaries. We may be required to act in ways that take us outside our comfort zone and move us deeply into vulnerability. Although the personal quest is a powerful place to begin, consider whether you might also be willing to be an ambassador of understanding.

As caring humans, we may choose to be involved in the quest for peace and justice. Yet our tactical approach must be uniquely right for us. We must grapple with injustices in our heart. We must recognize that peace and justice are, at the crux, spiritual issues. When we know this, our efforts toward legal or legislative change will be carried out with greater clarity and meaning.

Upping the ante is often revealed through addressing smaller issues first and then taking on the larger ones. Helen Keller was renowned for her stance on women's suffrage, labor rights, and socialism. Yet she began as a deaf and mute young girl. She was taught hand movements to communicate with tremendous focus, support, guidance, and firmness from her teacher, Annie Sullivan. Over time, Helen learned to speak, small sound by small sound.

She came to understand that great things are accomplished through small tasks completed consistently over time.

Maintaining and building peace, whether with your own money or through activism, must by its nature be an enduring practice, for there is much in the world that can cause us to lose our center of equanimity and to feel angry, outraged, or even despairing.

It has been said that maintaining peace is more difficult and challenging than maintaining war. I can attest to that observation. Even though I have lived and practiced peace for many years, I can still flash from a state of calm to a state of rage in a heartbeat. Rather than acting harshly, as I would have in the past, the difference now is that I almost always recognize when I've flashed to outrage and take myself by the hand to calm the fires of my emotions. Through allowing myself to feel the rage while not giving in to it—breathing through it and letting go—I can return to the grace of peace. With the calmness of peace, I think more clearly and act more effectively. It takes a deep and abiding commitment to continue the practice of peace. It takes even more clarity and focus to support others to find peace when they are not experiencing it.

As you grow in your commitment to living peace in every area of your life, you may discover some big, audacious actions you'll want to take. You might jump into these actions right away, or you may need time to build up to them. Some actions may seem contradictory to peace at first.

Imagine, for example, if Matthew needed to take physical protective measures to stop a teen who was high on drugs from stumbling into the street. Likely that teen would become angry or express some other negative emotion. Yet Matthew has shared that he keeps his eye steadfastly on his preferred outcome, which is the well-being of the teen, not on whether the teen will be angry with him.

Situations that raise strong feelings or emotions seem to make peace difficult to maintain. In these instances, you must have generosity of spirit toward yourself and others. When peace is absent, you may need to take measures to resume your commitment to it and refocus once again with clarity on the grace that peace can bring.

We can share our peace practices in varied difficult situations. Consider the board room at work or other mediation situations where you seek accord between two conflicting parties. You can take a stance for peace with money when people are fighting about it, whether it is you and your partner paying the bills or your kids fighting over a found dollar.

Upping the ante means supporting peace for others through your example: through how you approach your life and how you live each moment. Upping the ante is also seen through your practices of giving.

When you give of your wealth—of yourself, your concepts, your time, your energy, and your money—what you give can have significant impact. Whether you give toward actively stopping war, or to change the tenor of the work of legislative bodies, or to build greater harmony in the workplace, or to support other changemakers, you bring your own experience of peace to a whole new level.

Having peace in the midst of chaos is an exceptional capability and one well worth striving for.

Closing Notes

Our lives are meant to be enjoyed. To be lived with fullness and vitality. As humans, peace is far closer to our most natural state than war. We are meant to live in the full kaleidoscope of life experience, the delightful as well as the suffering, and each in its own timing.

Keeping ourselves in a state of struggle because of money is not what we came to this lifetime to do. For millennia of human existence, money as a form of currency did not even exist. Yes, there was barter, the exchange of goods and personal energy, but it was far more organic.

You have made a powerful choice in picking up this book and reading it. It is my intent that by conscientiously working and playing with the activities in this book and the *Make Peace with Money Workbook*, you have begun to discover a greater truth about your relationship with money. I trust you can see that you have the ability to change that relationship. Moreover, I trust that the clarity you've found is bringing you some greater measure of peace. To take peace even deeper, make the time to practice these activities consistently over time.

As you look with honesty at your monetary situation and face it courageously, you will gain the strength you need to make the necessary changes. This is the first step.

Shifting your thinking about money to become more positive and infusing your thinking with clarity, abundance, and gratitude is next. This will serve you well as you step into your vision for your life. As you fill your life and vision with purpose, you set a stage on which you can take clear and focused action.

Seeing the situation, becoming clear about what you want to change, and then taking action are the basics of this work. Surrounding yourself with peace will serve to anchor this work deeper within you and ensure successful results.

We are not here in this day and time just to make more and more money. At the end of our lives, our measure of success is not ultimately how many dollars we have earned. While there is nothing wrong at all with being financially successful, there is so much more to a life well lived.

We are here to love and support one another. We are here to contribute to living peaceful, civilized lives together—lives that are calm, fulfilling and have room for joy each day.

Evidence of nature's unceasing support surrounds us in every moment, whether you live by the ocean or near a meadow, in a bustling city or tucked into the forest. We already have enough, and we *are* enough; we have the potential as evolved, intelligent human beings to push forward the agenda of peace throughout all areas of our lives. And few areas need peace brought to it more than the area of money.

The struggle will continue as long as you choose to engage it. Peace is available to you in every moment and is waiting for you to come to it. In choosing to create a relationship with your money that is harmonious and satisfying, you will pave the way for peace to permeate your entire life: your health, your relationships, and your ability to feel joyful, supported, and at ease in the world.

Be gentle yet rigorous with yourself as you do this work. I have spent years working toward a life filled with peace with money.

If you approach the exercises in this book with a willing and courageous attitude, I know you will achieve success.

If you'll recall, my coach said to me, "Lorna, I can see you are not bad with money nor are you bad with numbers. There are simply some things you don't know yet."

Learning what you don't know yet will come about much more readily if you are willing to seek out and embrace the support of others. You can create a friendship circle of support, and there are excellent financial coaches, money professionals, and mentors to help should you find you want professional guidance.

And, above all, celebrate your achievements all along the way.

This book is the beginning of a powerful journey, the result of which is a gift to yourself that will last your entire life: the presence of monetary peace.

Peace with Money Activities

- Choose one area in your life, in your family, in your community, or on the world stage where you intend to make a difference toward peace.
- Write out the change you intend to work toward.
- Add the change you are working toward to your vision statement and read it every day for thirty days.
- Choose one small action, even a tiny one if needed, that you will take each day toward that peace.

Additional Resources

- Refer to the free *Make Peace with Money Workbook* at www.makepeacewithmoney.com, Lesson 14. Log in with the username *makepeacewithmoney* and the password *peace42*.

- *An Appeal to the World: The Way to Peace in a Time of Division* by the Dalai Lama and Franz Alt.

- *Mastering Life's Energies: Simple Steps to a Luminous Life at Work and Play* by Maria Nemeth.

THANK YOU

Are you interested in learning more? Would you like to join a community of people who are actively making peace with money themselves?

What are you waiting for?

Sign up now: www.makepeacewithmoney.com or visit our Facebook page here:
www.facebook.com/Make-Peace-with-Money-248829368609213

Thank you so much for choosing to come on this journey with me. I am glad that you are willing to pursue peace with money.

Please do not hesitate to connect with me if any questions come up about this book, or if you just want someone to chat with about this topic of making peace with money. I would be happy to hear from you.

Thanks again,

Lorna McLeod

A QUICK FAVOR PLEASE?

Before you go can I ask you for a quick favor?

Would you please post a review on Amazon for this *Make Peace with Money* book?

How delightful! I knew I could count on you.

Reviews are very important for authors, as they help us reach a greater audience with the work we are so passionate about.

Please take a quick minute to go to Amazon and leave this book an honest review. I promise it doesn't take long, but it can help this book reach more readers just like you.

Thank you so much for reading and for being part of the journey.

Lorna McLeod